# A FIRST COURSE IN WINE

## FROM GRAPE TO GLASS

# A FIRST COURSE IN WINE

## FROM GRAPE TO GLASS

*Dan Amatuzzi*

Race Point
PUBLISHING

*To Lourdes, for encouragingly reminding me
that a glass a day keeps the doctor away*

A division of Book Sales, Inc.
276 Fifth Avenue Suite 206
New York, New York 10001

RACE POINT PUBLISHING and the distinctive Race Point Publishing logo
are trademarks of Book Sales, Inc.

© 2013 by The Book Shop, Ltd.
7 Peter Cooper Road
New York, NY 10010

This 2013 edition published by Race Point Publishing by arrangement with
The Book Shop, Ltd.

EDITOR Catherine Nichols
DESIGN AND PHOTO RESEARCH Tim Palin Creative

ISBN-13: 978-1-937994-13-6

Printed in China

2 4 6 8 10 9 7 5 3 1

www.racepointpub.com

# CONTENTS

# Preface

In the spring of 2011, Joe Bastianich and I and our partners at Eataly started to consider who would staff the yet-unrealized 50,000-square-foot behemoth at 200 Fifth Avenue in New York City. The store would staff some 600 servers, cooks, stockers, cashiers, and Italian food experts on day one.

Dan Amatuzzi was then the wine director at Otto, our Greenwich Village enoteca and pizzeria. It was and remains a fast, high-volume restaurant with a wine list perhaps bigger than the menu might imply, about 1,000 wines over three full pages of tiny type in comparison to the single page of food offerings. In a short time, Amatuzzi had established a loyal following at Otto of wine-knowing staff members and of wine-loving (and drinking!) customers who had grown to appreciate his laid back, welcoming, and highly knowledgeable approach to wine drinking. He became the cerebral equivalent of the party implied by the wine, the food, and the fun scene that Otto had become.

We had little doubt who we would tap to conceive of and steer the wine program at Eataly, to foster a place where New Yorkers and tourists alike could drop by for a Pinot Grigio or Barbaresco in the piazza or sip a magnum of super Tuscan Sangiovese over an hours-long dinner at Manzo. Amatuzzi built the entire wine program at Eataly, from every sipping counter to each restaurant menu, from scratch.

In a short time, Amatuzzi has become the face of wine at Eataly and a top dog in the world of wine at our Batali & Bastianich Hospitality Group. He's changed the way we—our chefs and managers, our cooks and waiters—think about wine and wine service. And in turn, he's changed the way our customers drink.

Wine experts sometimes create a barrier to entry for prospective wine drinkers. This is generally because they are hungry to show the depth of their interest and knowledge. The more esoteric and refined Amatuzzi breaks that mold. He's a reformer, the future of wine service, the benevolent dictator with a soft spot for the unheralded heroes and lesser-known wines of true geo-specificity and value.

This, his first book, will make all who read it better wine drinkers, wine lovers, and wine consumers. It's a primer on the varietals, flavors, and personalities of the wine world past and present. More importantly, it allows the individual to better understand what there is to look for and to taste in a glass of wine.

Amatuzzi is also the reason New Yorkers have come to appreciate a mid-afternoon glass of *rosato* while shopping for dinner and contemplating the joy of existence in a world that is at once physical and transcendent...a fine line between infinity and nothingness....

That's a beautiful thing.

Share the joy and share a glass with a friend.

Mario Batali

*"In water one sees one's own face, but in wine one beholds the heart of another."*

– French proverb

# Introduction

I have no glorious story of how I got into wine. If anything, I haphazardly fell into it. My parents drank their fair share, but kept it simple and fun. I remember my extended family enjoying large meals together every Sunday, typically spaghetti with tomato sauce, or macaroni as we called it. Wine was a constant.

Like many before me, in college I chose to study in Europe for a semester, and it was during my time in Florence, Italy, that I saw wine in a different light. I liked how it brought people together—made them laugh, dance, and smile. I liked how it was complex and sophisticated, yet simple at its core. Determined to dig deeper, I focused a lot of my time and energy on wine after I returned home. I tried selling wine after college, but felt that I was limiting myself to only what was in the portfolio of the company. I wanted more. During my tenure as a wine representative, I met quite a few beverage directors and sommeliers working in New York's elite restaurants. They seemed cool. They wore suits, and were polished and professional, and they were up to their eyeballs in wine five to six days of the week, maybe seven depending upon what they did on their days off. I longed to join the ranks.

Restaurants are a tough business. One day you love them; the next you hate them. At the core of the service industry, you learn a lot about the human race and where exactly you fit in. Without any experience, I was destined to start at the bottom, regardless of my college degree. I began my journey as the stocker/polisher at Joe Bastianich and Mario Batali's restaurant, Babbo. The position is an industry term for glass and silverware polisher, one step up from dishwasher. While it may seem like an irrelevant job, I learned that polishing glasses is crucial to wine enjoyment, for a dirty wineglass can ruin the experience and possibly turn someone from wine altogether. I polished those glasses to a high shine, confident that each glass would bring a life-altering experience to the next person who used it.

I went on to fill other positions in other restaurants and earned my sommelier accreditation. I've tasted tens of thousands of wines throughout the journey, and if I've learned anything, it is that I'm still a student of wine. One lifetime is too short to know everything, but if you take it one wine at a time and keep it fun along the way, you'll go further than you've ever thought possible into the vast and beautiful world of wine. And you'll do so with a degree of finality and faith.

How do you define deliciousness? The answer is different for all of us. While there are some fundamentals about wine, remember that enjoying wine is an experience, and it is different for each and every one of us. With time will come confidence, but it is important to stick to your guns and be bold in your choices and how you approach wine. And most importantly, don't take it too seriously.

Dan Amatuzzi

# Part One

## Wine Basics

While there are many aspects to understanding wine, with just a few building blocks you can cover a lot of ground quickly. Having a basic understanding of how wine is made, how to taste it, and what separates one wine from the next will set the foundation for a life-long relationship with this coveted drink.

# What Is Wine?

In its most basic form wine is nothing more than fermented grape juice. Winemakers add yeast to crushed grapes, and the sugar in the juice turns into alcohol. A variety of methods can alter the profile of a wine, such as long skin maceration during the crushing process, aging in oak barrels, and blending different grapes together. Different grape varieties also produce wines with varying flavors and aromas.

## *Why aren't other fruits used to make wine?*

While other fruit juices are fermentable, their sugar ratios produce beverages that are usually too sweet and jammy. Grapes have a unique proportion of sugars and acids that enables all the sugar to be transferred into alcohol.

## *Is it possible to make wine from supermarket grapes?*

Table grapes sold in supermarkets are capable of making wine, but the flavors and aromas are less desirable than those that come from other species of grapes. Because table grapes are grown to maximize the quantity of berries with no regard to quality they're at the bottom of the totem pole for wine making.

## *How do I know which wines I'll like?*

Enjoying wine is a subjective process. There are many qualified and influential wine critics the world over, but the most important judge for evaluating wine is YOU. Don't be misled by what others say; let your senses guide you. Some things to focus on when evaluating a wine are:

- Body and color
- Aroma
- Flavor
- Finish

We'll analyze all of the above in greater detail, but thinking about these elements of a wine is crucial for determining your preferences.

*On average, it takes about 2½ pounds (1 kg) of grapes— or nearly 100 grapes—to make one bottle of wine.*

# The Different Types of Wine

There are six main categories of wine, all produced in slightly different ways.

**White Still:** Wine made by crushing grapes and separating the juice from the crushed skins.

**Red Still:** Wine made by crushing grapes and macerating the crushed skins for an extended period of time.

**Rosé Still:** Wine made by crushing grapes and macerating the crushed skins for a brief period of time. Also made by blending white and red wines together.

**Sparkling Carbonated:** Wine made by trapping carbon dioxide produced during alcoholic fermentation.

**Dessert:** Wine made by arresting fermentation and keeping some residual sugars, making the wines sweet and fruity.

**Fortified:** Wine that is higher in alcohol, caused by fortifying the wines with neutral-flavored spirits.

## Where should I start?

Begin by trying wines from one particular part of the world. Wines that come from the same area often resemble each other in the way of body, flavor, and sometimes price. If you begin in California, try a few different wines made from Chardonnay, Cabernet Sauvignon, and Merlot. If you like them all, keep digging and begin to seek out different producers of the grapes that you prefer. Afterwards, explore another part of the world and aim to see if you can find the same grapes grown.

If you dislike all the wines from one region, perhaps you're better suited to start with another part of the world. It is not that you'll never like wines from California, but you might have to work your way there in time. The more wines you taste, the more your palate develops, and you'll appreciate certain aspects of wine that previously went unnoticed.

## What makes a great wine?

While a winemaker makes many decisions that influence the final product, all wines begin with grapes, and the quality of the grapes is of utmost importance. The geography and elevation of the vineyard, the exposure to the sun, the density of the grapevines, how the vines are pruned, and the weather conditions all factor into how the grape will grow and mature on the vine.

Once the grapes are ripe, they're cut from the vine and brought to the winery. From here, the winemaker will decide how to produce the wine—but without high quality grapes, none of the decisions made in the winery will much matter.

## What determines the price of a wine?

Many factors determine a wine's price. The origin of the grapes, where it is made, how it is made (i.e. hand-harvested grapes vs. machine-harvested grapes), how it is marketed, and the popularity among critics are just a few factors that influence a wine's cost. Wines that are aged in oak barrels are also usually more expensive due to the high cost of barrels.

## Are more expensive wines always better?

Certainly not! The best way to develop your skills is to start simple and evaluate your likes and dislikes. Some of your favorite wines will be well within your budget. When buying wine, price doesn't always reflect quality.

## What about older wines?

The quality of a wine and the satisfaction it brings ultimately rests with you. Less than 1 percent of all the wine made every year is meant to age longer than five years, and most wines are best enjoyed within a few years of bottling.

## At which temperatures should wine be served?

Most enthusiasts believe the best way to enjoy sparkling and white wines is chilled, usually between 50° and 60° F (10° and 15° C), and red wines slightly warmer, between 60° and 70° F (15° and 20° C). Any cooler for both types and the fruit and aromas of the wine are suppressed and you could miss all the wine has to offer. Any warmer and the alcohol in the wine becomes more noticeable by a slight tingling and burning sensation in your nose. In these cases, the alcohol outweighs the floral and taste components of the wine, and once again, you could miss the enjoyable parts of the wine. However, these are just guidelines and the serving temperature of wine is another subjective topic of wine appreciation. If at the end of the day, you like your whites served at room temperate and your reds served with ice cubes…so be it!

## Are corked bottles superior to ones with screw caps?

Just as enjoying wines is subjective, winemakers choose closures based on what they believe is best for the wines. There's no reason to think a wine is cheap if it is closed with a screw cap or something other than a cork. There are plenty of high-end wines and high-quality wines that have non-cork closures.

*Are guests arriving any minute and you need to chill the wine? Pop the bottle in the freezer for ten minutes if it's red or 20 minutes if it's white or sparkling. You can also submerge the wine in an ice-water bath to drop the temperature in a flash.*

## Does drinking wine have any health benefits?

Wine is generally accepted to be a contributing factor to a long and healthy life—when consumed in moderation.

Drinking wine lowers bad cholesterol (LDL), which otherwise accumulates in arterial walls and leads to plaque, causing arteries to stiffen and blood pressure to rise. Wine also increases good cholesterol (HDL), helping to fend off heart disease.

Red wines absorb polyphenols and other antioxidants found in the skins of grapes. Polyphenols keep blood vessels flexible, lowering the risk of clotting. They also protect the immune system from the common cold.

Resveratrol is the most praised component of red wines. It helps moderate blood-sugar levels and lowers blood pressure. It has been shown to help keep the brain sharp by hampering Alzheimer's-inducing proteins from forming. Recently, resveratrol has been tested for fighting cancer, and so far the results have been encouraging. Researchers at the University of Virginia found that resveratrol obtained from drinking three to four glasses of red wine per week may be enough to starve nascent cancer cells.

Piceatannol is a compound our bodies convert from resveratrol, and it too, has benefits. It binds to insulin receptors of fat cells and stymies the formation of immature fat cells from forming.

The acids in wine aid in digestion. As we age, our bodies sometimes have trouble producing acids for this purpose, so wine is a helpful component for breaking down food molecules in our stomachs.

## It can't all be good for you, right?

Like many things in life, wine should be enjoyed in moderation. If abused, all the positives of wine are washed away. The most-cited health concern is liver disease.

If the body receives too much alcohol on a regular basis, the liver will have trouble filtering out the toxins. In the long run this can lead to liver failure.

Too much alcohol can also weaken heart muscles and lead to cardiomyopathy, a condition where the heart fails to pump blood around the body as well as it should.

People with a history of migraines are often advised to limit their consumption of wine because the histamines and tannin found in wine can trigger re-occurring headaches.

Tyramine is an amino acid found in wine that causes cerebral blood vessels to contract. Painful headaches can occur the next day when the blood vessels reopen. Consuming water and having something in your stomach can help the body absorb tyramine.

Weight gain can be another drawback to over-consumption. Wine contains "empty calories" – calories that lack nutrients – which help pack on the pounds if prolonged enjoyment of wine isn't matched by sufficient exercise.

Worldwide, the French consume the most wine, downing almost 56 liters (15 gallons) per person per year. That's about a glass of wine every day. By contrast, the average drinker in the United States drinks a glass of wine once a week.

A 2010 study of more than 4,000 people found that those who drank a glass of wine every week for one year were 40 percent less likely to come down with a common cold.

A 6-ounce (175-ml) glass of wine contains about 120 calories.

# Know Your Grapes 101

Just a handful of grape varieties grown throughout the world produce wine. When grown in different soils and climates, however, these grapes yield a multitude of aromas and flavors. Here are the usual suspects that line most aisles in the wine shop.

## Major White Grape Varieties

### Alvarinho
*(ahl-vah-RHEE-nyoh)*

**Most famous for wines from:**
Spain; Portugal

**Flavor profile:**
apricot, peach, cream, citrus

A noble white grape that produces Portugal's principal white wine, Vinho Verde. It is also planted in Spain and makes bracing and fresh white wines, ideal for shellfish and starter dishes, notably in Galicia. The skins are thicker than normal, so only a small amount of juice can be extracted from them or else the wines may take on too much tannin and lose their fresh and clean appeal.

### Chardonnay
*(shar-dohn-NAY)*

**Most famous for wines from:**
Burgundy and Champagne, France; California; Australia

**Flavor profile:**
apple, pear, herbaceous, grapefruit, lemon, melon

The grape grows throughout the world and makes plenty of dull and unexciting wines, but when grown with care, Chardonnay is responsible for some of the greatest white wines made anywhere in the world. It is also one of the most important grapes for sparkling wine production.

### Chenin Blanc
*(SHEN-ihn BLANHK)*

**Most famous for wines from:**
Loire Valley, France; South Africa

**Flavor profile:**
rich, fruit-forward, honey, pear, ripe tropical fruits

High natural sugars make many of the wines seem rich and unctuous compared to other white wines. While there are some very good dry versions of the grape, there are just as many high-end and collectable off-dry, dessert, and sparkling wines. When overripe, the wines can taste flabby and fat, but when made well, they can rival most any other white wines in complexity.

*Chardonnay grapes from New Zealand.*

## Gewürztraminer

*(guh-VERTZ-tra-meen-er)*

**Most famous for wines from:**
Germany; France; Austria; Italy; California

**Flavor profile:**
rose-pedal, lychee, Asian spices, clove, nutmeg

Holding the title for most difficult grape to pronounce, Gewürztraminer is considered one of the more aromatic white grape varieties. Originating in northern Italy in the town of Tramin, it is often a recommended pairing with Asian-inspired dishes. Its name is derived from the German term *gewürz*, meaning "spiced." Due to the grapes' dark yellow and pink skins, the wines are usually darker in color than most other whites with golden raisin and peach notes.

## Grüner Veltliner

*(GREW-ner FELT-lean-er)*

**Most famous for wines from:**
Austria; California; Germany; Italy

**Flavor profile:**
almond, flint, lemongrass, melon, spearmint, herbaceous

The grape is Austria's most widely planted variety. Given Austria's cool climate, the wines are crisp, pale in color, and lean, refreshing, and racy. Grüner, as it is commonly called, has been planted in other parts of the world, but is still largely centered in Austria and parts of Germany and northern Italy.

## Muscat/Moscato

*(MUH-skaht)/(mow-SKA-toe)*

**Most famous for wines from:**
France; Italy; California

**Flavor profile:**
honeysuckle, elderflower, peach, pear

There are numerous strains and offshoots of Muscat that have promulgated throughout the world, but the trademark aromas and flavors are hard to miss. Either sweet and syrupy or slightly sparkling, this grape is the dominant variety used throughout the world to make dessert wines.

## Pinot Gris/Pinot Grigio

*(PEE-noh GREE)/*
*(PEE-noh GREEJ-e-oh)*

**Most famous for wines from:**
Italy; France; Oregon; Hungary; Romania

**Flavor profile:**
lemon, lime, herbaceous, bright, zesty

Most expressions are steely, flinty, and fresh. When overproduced, the grape can yield wines very tart and unbalanced. It has become ubiquitous in the Italian section of wine lists and in wine shops, and is the second most-frequently ordered wine by the glass in restaurants in the United States. The skins of the grape are graying and pinkish hued and sometimes the wines are made with extended skin contact, resulting in pink and copper-toned wines. Italians label this style *ramato*, translating to "copper."

*Pinot Gris grapes.*

## Riesling

*(REEZ-ling)*

**Most famous for wines from:**
Germany; France; Australia; Austria

**Flavor profile:**
zesty, orange, petrol, lanolin, apricot

The grape is the signature "cool-climate" grape. Enthusiasts hail its acidic profile. Even when the wine is made with residual sugar, the bright character and zippiness make any and all expressions very food friendly. It is native to Germany where it is been cultivated for more than 2,000 years.

## Sauvignon Blanc

*(SOH-vee-nyawn BLAHNGK)*

**Most famous for wines from:**
Loire Valley, France; New Zealand; Australia; California

**Flavor profile:**
kiwi, tropical fruits, herbaceous, freshly cut grass, jalapeño, flint, smoke

Also called Fumé Blanc, hinting to the smoky and flinty notes commonly found in the wine. The term, coined by Robert Mondavi, references the appellation, or grape-growing region, in France, Pouilly-Fumé, where Sauvignon Blanc reigns supreme. In Europe, the wines tend to be lighter and more bracing with fresh and clean flavors, whereas in New Zealand and Australia, the wines are a bit heavier, richer, and offer more fruit and aromas.

## Trebbiano

*(treh-bee-AHN-noh)*

**Most famous for wines from:**
Italy; France; California

**Flavor profile:**
grapefruit, dried hay, melon

Widely planted throughout the world, especially Europe. It is easy to cultivate and has high yields, making it the ideal work-horse grape for many blended wines. In France, it is used to make the famous grape brandies, Armagnac and Cognac, and is also used to make brandy throughout other parts of the world.

## Viognier

*(vee-ohwn-YAY)*

**Most famous for wines from:**
Rhône Valley, France; southern France; Australia; California

**Flavor profile:**
lush, floral, peach, honey, banana

Considered by many to be the most aromatic white grape variety in the world. The wines from Condrieu in France are the most noble and decadent expressions of the grape. Some producers choose to leave the grapes on the vine a bit longer than other grapes, to generate higher sugars and produce unctuous dry and off-dry wines. The vines produce less grapes than other varieties, and it's very susceptible to disease, so plantings are few and far between.

*Sauvignon Blanc grapes.*

California

of the more
ows throughout
ome from
ome into its
underripe,
having "bell-
st varietal
the Loire Valley
region. It is also
ere it is often
and Merlot,

## Cabernet Sauvignon

*(KAH-behr-nay SOH-vee-nyawn)*

**Most famous for wines from:**
Bordeaux, France; Australia; California; Italy; Spain; South America

**Flavor profile:**
cassis, plum, blackberry, eucalyptus

The grape is responsible for putting California reds on the winemaking map, and it is still the prized and most-profitable grape variety to grow in Napa and Sonoma. It is also the dominant grape used to make wines on the left bank of Bordeaux. The high tannin and acidity of the grape give wines unparalleled aging potential. The most popular red wine in the world, it is grown in what seems every potential winemaking country.

## Carmenère *(car-min-EHR)*

**Most famous for wines from:**
Chile; France; Italy

**Flavor profile:**
blueberry, geranium, cherry, black olive

Originally one of the minor grapes of Bordeaux (sometimes called the sixth grape of Bordeaux), it has found a new home in Chile. It grows especially well in the high-elevation and coastal vineyards. It produces silky wines with lush dark fruit flavors, best enjoyed in their youth.

## Corvina *(kohr-VEE-nuh)*

**Most famous for wines from:**
Veneto, Italy

**Flavor profile:**
fig, cherry, leather, prune, raisin

Used to make the wines in Valpolicella in northern Italy. Sometimes the grapes are dried before they're pressed to make wine, in which case the wines are called Amarone della Valpolicella. These wines are high in alcohol, with concentrated flavors of prunes, figs, and herbs. The high alcohol content is offset by the high tannin and bitter flavors, hence the name "Amarone," stemming from the Italian word amaro, meaning bitter.

*Cabernet Sauvignon grapes from Bordeaux, France.*

## Gamay *(gah-MAY)*

**Most famous for wines from:**
Beaujolais, France

**Flavor profile:**
raspberry and bright red fruits, banana, peach

Naturally low in tannin and high in acidity, the grape makes light and easy-drinking wines, although there are some high-end bottlings that come from the top-designated vineyards within Beaujolais. It is planted in other parts of the world, but used in small quantities to add freshness to blended wines.

## Grenache/Garnacha *(gruh-NAHSH)*

**Most famous for wines from:**
Spain; France; Italy; Australia; California

**Flavor profile:**
blackberry, plum, liquorice, leather, tar, spice

Grenache thrives in hot and dry climates. The root structure is very strong and the vines can be planted in very windy areas to sustain the periodic gusts. Natural high-sugars in the grape translate to higher-alcohol wines, usually very powerful and gripping with tannin. It is the most widely planted black-grape variety in Spain, and is also planted in many other hot growing regions around the world. In France, it is grown mostly in the south and is used in the famous and age-worthy wines of the Rhône Valley where it is blended with Syrah.

## Malbec *(mahl-BEHK)*

**Most famous for wines from:**
France; Argentina; Italy; California

**Flavor profile:**
black cherry, mint, black olive, toffee, blueberry

Grown throughout France, most notably in Bordeaux, Loire Valley, and Cahors, it produces inky, rich, and tannic wines. In Argentina's valleys and plains, the grape has become the most popular variety. Argentinean styles of the grape usually have silkier tannin profiles and juicy blueberry fruit flavors.

## Merlot *(mehr-LOH)*

**Most famous for wines from:**
Bordeaux, France; California;
Washington State; Italy

**Flavor profile:**
plum, blackberry, currant, herbaceous, mint

Grown extensively in Bordeaux, where it is usually used as a blending grape that adds color and body to wines. It grows well in damp soils like clay and makes approachable wines rich in color and fruitiness.

## Nebbiolo *(neh-b'YOH-loh)*

**Most famous for wines from:**
Piedmont, Italy

**Flavor profile:**
cranberry, mushroom, herbaceous, toffee, truffles, violet

Its name is taken from the Italian word *nebbia*, meaning "fog," a reference to the habitual fog that permeates the valleys of the Piedmont. Loaded with tannin and acidity, the grape produces some of Italy's most-prized and age-worthy wines. Wines are light in color and are extremely powerful, tannic, and gripping in their youth. Over time, they develop incredibly complex aromas and flavors of truffles, mushrooms, dried fruits, and cowhide.

*Nebbiolo grapes from Piedmont, Italy.*

## Pinotage *(PEE-noh-TAHJ)*

**Most famous for wines from:**
South Africa; California; New Zealand

**Flavor profile:**
floral, herbaceous, raspberry, cherry

A genetically produced grape made by crossing Pinot Noir and Cinsault. South Africans refer to the grape as hermitage, thus the name Pinotage. It produces light to medium-bodied wines reminiscent of young fruity Pinot Noir wines. Pinotage plantings outside South Africa are spotty, but can be interesting when found.

## Pinot Noir *(PEE-noh NWAHR)*

**Most famous for wines from:**
Burgundy, France; Oregon; New Zealand

**Flavor profile:**
mushroom, raspberry, violet, lavender, game, fig, prune

Considered one of the most difficult grapes to grow. It requires long, cool growing climates, and the skins are thin and are prone to rot and other diseases. Wines are never too full in color, but are powerful and complex. Young Pinot Noir wines usually exhibit fruity flavors of cherries, plums, and raspberries. Older wines take on more earthy, mushroom, leather, and tobacco notes. Enthusiasts can spend a lifetime (and a fortune) nitpicking the differences between vineyards in Burgundy, France, where the grape is used to make red wines. There are plenty of other great expressions of Pinot Noir made throughout the world, but Burgundy is the benchmark to which all others are compared. It is also used to make sparkling wines in Champagne, France, and other parts of the world.

## Sangiovese *(san-gio-VAY-zeh)*

**Most famous for wines from:**
Italy; California

**Flavor profile:**
leather, tar, cherry, raspberry

The main grape of central Italy, especially in Chianti and also in Montalcino, where it is referred to as Brunello. Most wines are meant for early consumption, but some wines, especially from Montalcino, can age for decades. The success of Sangiovese in Italy has prompted more plantings throughout California and also South America.

## Syrah *(see-RAH)*

**Most famous for wines from:**
France; Australia; California

**Flavor profile:**
tar, spice, pepper, blackberry, currant, plum, cigar box, tobacco

Also referred to as Shiraz, the grape makes some of the most powerful and richest wines. Thick skins rich in color pigments translate to heavy, full-bodied, and alcoholic wines. In France, the grape is grown throughout the Rhône Valley and is the main variety in many of the best appellations including Cornas, Côte-Rôtie, and Châteauneuf-du-pape. In Australia, it is responsible for many of the best wines from the Barossa Valley. The wines are intense, big, and structured, rich in spicy fruit and power.

## Tempranillo *(tem-prah-NEE-yoh)*

**Most famous for wines from:**
Spain; Argentina

**Flavor profile:**
strawberry, spice, tobacco, rose, clove

Spain's most important grape variety, it is grown throughout the country and is the dominant grape in most of the major appellations including Rioja and Ribera del Duero. When young, the wines are lush and juicy, and with age they take on aromas of dried fruits and spices.

## Zinfandel *(ZIHN-fuhn-dehl)*

**Most famous for wines from:**
California; South Africa; Australia; Italy

**Flavor profile:**
anise, spice, black cherry, plum, raisin, fig

Considered the principal grape of the United States, in part to the lack of extensive vineyards in other countries, it grows well in hot and arid climates. Wines are full-bodied and high in alcohol but balanced by firm tannin. It has been proved to be genetically the same grape as Italy's southern variety Primitivo.

# Part Two

---

# Seasons of the Vine

Growing grapes is not an easy task. Any time throughout the year a variety of uncontrollable obstacles can arise, including frost, hail, drought, fire, earthquakes, or landslides. Equally dangerous are vine and grape diseases or problems caused by insects or animals. It is hardly surprising, then, that wine sometimes costs an arm and a leg. Thankfully, winemakers have learned how best to use breakthroughs in science and technology to produce award-winning wine. None of their skills and training will be of help, however, if the months leading up to the harvest season are riddled with any of the aforementioned setbacks and the vineyards fail to produce useable grapes.

## Winter

In the northern hemisphere, the season of the vine begins in the winter months when vineyard managers walk up and down the rows of vines cutting back any remaining leaves or shoots from the previous year. In February or March, the vine, triggered by rising soil temperature, begins "weeping." In this process, the vine's roots collect water and the resulting sap is expelled through the ends of the cane, or stem. Weeping signals the winemaker to begin pruning the vine for spring.

## Spring

About thirty days later, buds appear on the vine, the first sign of leaves. If the vine grows in a cooler soil like clay, this step will likely occur a few weeks later than if the vine grows in a lighter soil such as sand or gravel.

Within eight weeks of bud break, the vine produces embryo flowers, which eventually become grapes. At this point in the cycle, soil temperature is crucial, so the heat-retention capacity of the soil is pivotal for the vine to grow properly. From this point on, any inclement or treacherous weather phenomena (wildfire, hail, floods, erosion) can damage the grapes. Should any of these occur, the grapes may still grow on the vine but will fail to ripen. In other cases, the grapes will cease to grow any further. Both scenarios result in lost production.

## Summer

By June, the grapes increase in size as the acid levels increase. For the next sixty days, weather plays a pivotal role in proper grape development. Perhaps counterintuitively, it is widely believed that the best wines are produced from grapevines that have to struggle to survive. Mostly this "struggling" refers to a lack of water. From the time of fruit set until harvest, drier conditions are preferred. When vines are deprived of easy access to water, vine vigor slows, and instead of developing more leaves and shoots, the plant allocates all its resources towards developing the fruit. On the other hand, too much rain will cause the vine to swell with water, diluting the fruit and diminishing the potential to make great wine. In many of the premier winemaking zones in the northern hemisphere, June, July, and August are extremely dry with light and sporadic rainfall.

Green harvesting is a subtle pruning and cutting process often conducted in the weeks or months before the grapes will be picked. Vineyard workers walk up and down the rows cutting leaves and some of the grape bunches in hopes that the grapes remaining on the vine will get all the nutrients and resources the vine has to offer. The less grapes remaining on the vine, the greater amount of nutrients each grape will receive.

## Harvest

In August, about 150 days after the buds first appear on the vine, the grapes' sugar levels rapidly increase, and if the grape is a black-skinned grape like Cabernet Sauvignon or Merlot, the pigments in the skins change from green to violet. This is caused by tissue softening, decreases in tartaric and malic acid, increases in fructose levels, and the development of aroma compounds. Determining when to pick the ripened grapes is a crucial part of the harvesting process. Winemakers can use instruments and science to help identify grapes with ideal levels of acids and sugars; however, a winemaker's intuition is still a coveted tool. If the winemaker picks before the grapes are ripe, the finished wine may be overly acidic and taste "green," "sharp," and "tart." On the other hand, if the winemaker waits too long, then catastrophic early frosts, freezing rain, or hailstorms can wipe out vineyards in a matter of minutes.

The grape harvest is a spiritual time in a winemaker's life. All the labor of toiling in the vineyards and working with nature's offerings has created grapes that will now be processed into wine. With a little more luck, all will go well in the winery.

*New vineyards usually require three to four years to establish a strong root system capable of producing enough fruit to make wine. Even so, fruit from a young vine never makes great wine. A grapevine needs to be much older before it produces grapes capable of making complex wines. Wineries sometimes blend grapes from older vines and grapes from younger vines to make balanced and consistent wines year after year.*

*Grape harvesting and winemaking depicted in the Tomb of Nakht during the Eighteenth Dynasty. Ca. 1400-1390 B.C.*

# Understanding the Vine

Most of us will never work in a vineyard, but the energy and love that go into a vine shouldn't go unnoticed. Vineyard managers and winemakers put a great deal of attention into the health and lifecycle of their precious crop. Sometimes a winemaker will disclose the way the vines were treated, either on the winery's website or even on the back label of the bottle itself, so being familiar with the terminology is key.

## Where did grapes originate?

Grapes were cultivated as early as 6000 B.C. and most probably originated in the Caucasus Mountains, in present day Georgia, Russia, Armenia, and Azerbaijan. Over the course of history, vines spread eastward and westward. As vines were planted in new climates and soils, genetic mutations occurred as the plant acclimated to its foreign surroundings. Over the course of 8,000 years, and with a little help from humans transporting the vines from place to place, different grape species propagated and today we're blessed with a variety of vine species.

Since grapevines have low agronomic needs, they were commonly planted in poorer soils and on hillsides while farmers used the richer soils for grains and grazing purposes. Grapevines also have superior regenerative properties. Their ease of growing and their fortitude made them popular candidates to bring along when civilization upped and moved.

## When was the first wine made?

Putting years of work into vineyards to produce wine was contradictory to most nomadic habits. Despite their existence, vines never made a serious impact in the world for quite some time. Grapevines have long been noted in historical documents dating as far back as 7,000 years, yet historians believe that the first intentional attempt at winemaking occurred 5,000 years ago during the reign of King Udimu in Egypt.

Commercial wines first appeared close to large cities where socioeconomic conditions enabled a market to grow. It wasn't until the mid-1600s that the idea of a wine from a certain place could be marketed and sold as a unique item, distinctly different from others in taste and consequently superior in value. Château Haut-Brion in Bordeaux, France, was the first producer to label and market its own wines. Thanks to a bustling trade relationship with Great Britain, the wines from this château and the other châteaux from southern France eventually became a much-desired commodity, and more Bordeaux châteaux properties sprang up in the 1700s. They've been relevant ever since.

*The first known reference to a specific vintage was made by Roman scientist Pliny the Elder, who rated the wines of 121 B.C. "of the highest excellence."*

*Throughout history, wine always had a place on the table since the preserving qualities of alcohol made it safer to consume, while drinks like milk and water were prone to disease and spoilage.*

## How did winemaking develop?

Around the same time, sulfur dioxide was discovered to be an effective agent against infection and spoilage. Wine was made in the fall, and had a short life span of about one year before the effects of oxidation turned the wine to vinegar. With sulfur-treated oak barrels, the quality of wine rapidly increased and the idea of long-term aging potential entered the fray, a concept that now drives the high-end segment of the wine trade.

The production of glass bottles also changed the future for wine. Prior to glass bottles, wine was sold and transported in wood barrels or tanks, which allowed oxygen in and made the wines short-lived. With glass bottles, wine lasted longer and a demand for better products emerged.

The ease and strength of glass bottles also gave rise to the popularity of producing sparkling wines, which are produced by trapping carbon dioxide during fermentation. Once Louis Pasteur defined the role of yeast and the consequential conversion of sugar into alcohol, enthused winemakers had all the tools they needed to take the next steps towards commercial production.

## What is terroir?

While there is no exact translation for this French term, the basic idea is that grapes grown in certain geographic locations, such as Burgundy, France, and Mosel, Germany, are unlike grapes grown anywhere else. *Terroir* is the summation of how a vine behaves and how the finished wine tastes. Within this framework, there are numerous variables that affect the final outcome. Some of the major ones follow.

## Soil

Many different soil types and many different elements affect vine growth. Thus, there is no simple equation for choosing which grapes to cultivate. The most important factors for wine production are soil temperature, water retention, and nitrogen uptake. Soils such as sand and gravel drain quickly, resulting in warmer soil temperatures. This induces earlier ripening of the fruit. Soils such as clay retain water and are generally cooler throughout the year. This delays bud break and flowering in the spring, resulting in a lengthy ripening process in the fall. Vineyard managers use this logic to map out grape selection, as certain varieties take to different soil types kindly, but not so well to others.

## Rain and Water

The minimum amount of rainfall per year needed for grape development is ten inches. Any less and the vines may shut down and fail to produce grapes, or worse, they'll perish. If there is a lack of nitrogen in the soil, vineyard managers can add organic nutrients to irrigation water to help subsidize the void. If there is too much nitrogen, they can grow cover crops such as clover fields and barley, which consume nitrogen and add enriching elements back into the soil for the vine to feed upon. Potassium uptake is also cited as an influential factor in grape development as it aids in cell osmosis and the crucial transfer of sugars between the skin cells and the flesh.

In summary, great winemakers insist that the flavors and aromas of their wines are already present in the grapes. All that they do is step aside and allow the wines to speak for themselves. They believe that the vine receives its strength and character from the area in which it grows. Given two similar places of land, surely the soil types, access to rain and water, elevation, and aspect of the grapevines will differentiate the two. This is the underlying meaning of *terroir*.

*Steep hills and vineyards in Friuli Venezia Giulia, Italy.*

## *Why do certain grapes grow all over the world and others only in one place?*

Some grape varieties tend to grow better in particular soil types. For example, Syrah and Zinfandel grapes prefer sandy soil and hot climates, while Pinot Noir grows best in pebbly soil in cool climates. While soil type may help a winemaker decide which grape to grow, winemakers are experimenting and pushing the boundaries of which grapes to grow where. The future is bright for wine enthusiasts eager to try their favorite grapes from new spots in the world.

## *How do aspect and slope affect winemaking?*

Aspect refers to the location of vineyards in respect to the sun's path. In the northern hemisphere, the prime vineyards are planted on hillsides facing south, maximizing the exposure to solar rays. The same holds true for the southern hemisphere, as vineyards on northern-facing slopes receive more of the benefits of direct sunlight. Although the extra exposure in these prime vineyard spots may be only a matter of minutes every day, throughout an entire year this can add up to more than 30 or 40 additional hours of sunlight. It may not sound like much, but it can make or break proper grape development in certain years. The minimum hours of sunlight per year for a vine to fully grow and produce useable fruit is 1,300 hours; however most winemaking areas receive substantially more.

Slopes can be advantageous for this reason, but they are also precarious. As elevation rises every 330 feet, temperature falls by 1.8° F, a concept called lapse effect. Since cooler temperatures equate to longer growing seasons, vineyard managers must be wary of the different ripening schedules of the grapes in a vineyard characterized by extreme changes in elevation.

The type of grape variety also helps dictate the position of the vineyards and where exactly on the land those grapes are grown. For example, some grapes ripen more effectively when exposed to only the morning sun and are shielded by leaves throughout the rest of the day. In many cases, white grapes are exposed to the sun in the late morning hours and then the leaves are positioned so that the grapes are sheltered throughout the afternoon when the sun's rays are generally more potent. This kind of vineyard management enables winemakers to optimize the variety of grapes grown and maximize the quality of these grapes.

## How do lakes, rivers, and oceans play a role in winemaking?

Most of the world's premier winemaking zones are located in close proximity to bodies of water. This is due in part to two reasons of equal importance.

First, water helps moderate the temperatures in nearby areas. A large body of water can affect the temperatures of a vineyard as far as 25 miles away. As air travels over large bodies of water, it cools or warms to according to the temperature of the water. If it is the dead of summer and the water temperature is less than the air temperature, the air that blows over the water is cooled, which then permeates through the vineyards and helps mitigate the intense heat. Likewise, if it's cooler in spring or late autumn, as air travels over warmer bodies of water, the air in the vineyard receive some warmth, which helps keep the grapes from freezing. Vines that grow on the banks of lakes and rivers also benefit from the sunlight that reflects off the water, helping to induce photosynthesis.

Waterways were once a major part of the wine trade. Before the advent of rail, truck, and air transportation, waterways were the only way to get premium goods such as herbs, spices, silks, and wine from their origin to a marketplace. Hundreds of years ago, wine barrels were commonplace in the hulls of many mercantile ships sailing the seas and river systems of Europe and Asia.

# Vine Species

Vines and winemakers share a lasting and sacred bond. As Austrian winemaker Heidi Schröck so eloquently states: "My inspiration is the vine itself. With its powerful roots it collects the life force which comes from deep below the surface. As the root system grows deeper and more complex, the wine becomes more interesting and multifaceted. Being in the vineyard helps me to understand nature and to know my own boundaries."

Grapes mature differently on the vine. Some end up proportionately higher in different levels of acids and sugars than others, making vineyard management an integral part of the winemaking process. Many wineries employ teams of acclaimed scientific professionals solely dedicated to guiding the vineyard to provide evenly ripened fruit bunches.

Vine species differ mostly by the shape and color of the grapes, seeds, canes, and tendrils. The geographic locations where they thrive and their flowering and fruiting properties are also quite different. Almost all of the grapes we are accustomed to belong to the genus *vitis* and the species *vinifera*.

Within each species there are different varieties. Grapes like Cabernet Sauvignon, Riesling, Merlot, Chardonnay, and the rest of the gang are all different varieties, also referred to as "cultivars," within the *vinifera* species. The superiority of their flowering capabilities (which eventually become the coveted grapes) and the ensuing fruit properties and flavor components of the finished wine compared to other species gives them the edge when it comes to making wine.

While these grapes make excellent wines, they are rather difficult to eat directly off the vine. The pulp is tightly wound around the seeds, making it difficult to enjoy the flavors. If you visit a vineyard, don't be surprised if you're disappointed when eating these grapes directly off the vine.

While most of the world's winemaking grapes we're familiar with are part of the *vinifera* species, other species shouldn't go neglected. In fact, if it weren't for *vitis labrusca* and *vitis rupestris*, wine as we know it today wouldn't exist. Not only do the disease-resistant rootstocks of American vines *vitis labrusca* help form the foundation of many vineyards, these species of grapes can also make favorable wines. They may not make the headlines in magazines, and you won't find them much in the more famous winemaking areas, but *vitis labrusca* grapes such as Niagara, Isabella, and Catawba are catching on, both with winemakers and consumers who are eager to expand their horizons.

Within the broad spectrum of grapes, there are three major divisions:

**Varieties** Pure grapes belonging to one specific grape species, such as Cabernet Franc, Merlot, Concord, Catawba.

**Crosses** Generally referred to grapes that are intentionally created using two grapes of the same species. One of the more famous crosses is Müller-Thurgau, developed by the German scientist of the same name, H. Müller-Thurgau. In 1882, he crossed Riesling and Sylvaner (or Chasselas) grapes.

**Hybrids** Produced by combining two grapes from two different species, such as Baco Noir, Chambourcin, Maréchal Foch, Seyval Blanc.

## How do winemakers control the grapevines?

There are many ways growers can influence both the quality and quantity of the grapes. Some vines are grown in loose rows so as not to crowd the vines. Others are planted close together to benefit from the canopies shading the grapes throughout the vineyard. In some cases, the branches of the vine are trained along wire trellises to help the grower position where the fruit bunches will grow. For some grape varieties, the ideal position is higher up on the vine to shield the grapes from ground frost. Other times, the grapes are best grown lower on the vine closer to the ground to benefit from heat and sunlight that reflects off the soil. It all depends on where the vineyard is located, which grape varieties are grown, and how the grower intends for the vineyard to mature.

The vine is also pruned and trimmed throughout the year. By pruning, growers can initially control where the grape bunches will form and then eliminate bunches and leaves if the vine is too productive. A winemaker's preferences for vine positioning, trellising, and pruning will dictate how much fruit the vine bears, and ultimately, how much wine will be produced.

*Grapes are unique in that of all the fruits gathered by humans, only grapes store carbohydrates in the form of soluble sugars. Others store carbohydrates as starch and pectin, nutrients that are not fermentable by wine yeasts.*

*Scientists estimate there are more than two thousand grape species and nearly 15,000 different varieties of grapes.*

*Pruning the vine gives a winemaker more control over fruit quality and quantity.*

# The Lifecycle of a Vineyard

When growers decide where to plant vineyards, they must consider soil depth, chemical makeup, and drainage and/or erosion potential. Choosing the initial rootstock is of utmost importance, for it will provide the backbone to the grapevine. Most rootstocks are grown using mature canes from the mother-vine, which are then planted in nurseries to grow in ideal conditions. Scions from *vinifera* species are then taken from existing vines and grafted onto the rootstock. The new vines are planted in earth in the early spring once conditions are favorable. Once planted, it takes a grapevine about three years before it bears enough fruit to produce wine. The end goal is to have a strong root system that is resistant to disease, while producing fruit that will provide the desired aromas and flavors for the finished wine.

The fruit from a young grapevine isn't always ideal for wine making. While it may produce many grapes, the resulting wines are often regarded as simple, linear, monotone or easy going, reflecting the innocence and naivety of its grapes. Like a baby taking its first steps, they're not always the most graceful, but we can appreciate the effort that goes into them. It isn't until 15 to 40 years that the vines really hit their stride, and the quality of the fruit grows by leaps and bounds while the quantity of grapes is also high. The wines produced using grapes from older vines are often more complex. After 40 to 70 years, the vine grows less

*This grapevine's age is revealed by its thick and dried base and canes.*

productive and the quantity of grape production thins out. Just as a man will appreciate each and every hair on the top of his aging head, so does the winemaker cherish each and every grape from an old vine. The vine is entering a wearing-out process. It will continue to produce grapes every year as long as it is in the ground and as long as it is pruned and cared for (and assuming the weather is favorable), but the reliability of the quantity of fruit will vary. Much care and attention goes into tending these oldies but goodies.

At this point in a vine's lifecycle, the farmer is now faced with a choice. Rip up the vineyards and replant with younger and new vines and restart the cycle or let the vine continue to grow and become a relic of sorts.

Larger estates often have various parcels of lands with grapevines of varying ages. One part may be devoted to younger vines of 10 to 30 years. Another parcel may contain older vines, ranging from 30 to 60 years and yet another parcel of incredibly old vines, 70 years and older. This variety gives winemakers a few options.

They can produce different wines using grapes sourced depending upon the age of the vines. Consequently, we see these delineations in the marketplace. Some wines are labeled "New Vine" or "Vigne Nouve" (Italian) or "Vinas Nuevas" (Spanish), and so on. These wines are usually priced lower, released earlier, and are meant to be the most approachable of the lineup. We also see terms such as "Old Vine," "Vecchie Vigne" (Italian), or "Vieilles Vignes" (French) on wine labels. These wines are usually the winery's most important products and are seen as wines for special occasions and worthy of cellaring. They are usually more expensive and are aged at the winery before release. (While this type of labeling may be helpful for producers to delineate their wines, there is no international standard for what constitutes young or old vines, so this type of advertising can be somewhat misleading to the newbie wine drinker.)

*Montepulciano d'Abruzzo produced from vigne nouve, or young vines.*

*Pinot Noir produced from old vines in the New York's Finger Lakes region.*

# What Diseases Are Grapevines Susceptible to?

A grapevine is susceptible to a variety of diseases and pests, many of which will either render the vine useless or kill it outright. Some of the most relevant diseases and their remedies are summarized below.

| Disease | Symptoms and Effects on Vine | Remedy |
| --- | --- | --- |
| Black Rot | Fungal disease causing pitted leaves and discolored grapes; results in premature ripening of the fruit. Eventually the grapes shrivel on the vine and turn a brownish-black color. | Bordeaux Mixture (copper sulfites and unsalted lime). |
| Bitter Rot | Fungal disease that results in bitter-tasting fruit when picked at harvest and discoloration of the berries. | Spraying with fungicides. |
| Gray Rot | Fungal disease that spoils the grapes (negative side of the rot *botrytis cinera*). | None. |
| Leaf-Roll Virus | Visible by downward-curving leaf edges. Affects sugar accumulation in the fruit. | Replanting of vineyards with disease-free rootstocks. |
| Powdery Mildew (oidium) | Attacks green parts of vines including stems, grapes, and shoots. Covers with a grayish film. Fruit bunches break and bleed. | Copper sulfate sprays. |
| Downy Mildew | White patches form on underside of leaves. Defoliation occurs and vine withers. | Copper sulfate sprays. |
| Pierce's Disease | Bacteria carried by insects called, sharpshooters. Blocks the water supply of the vine. | Copper sulfate sprays. |
| Coulure | The failure of grapes to fully develop due to extended rains or cool temperatures during flowering. | None. |
| Phylloxera | Degenerates the root system. | Replant vineyards with phylloxera-resistant rootstocks. |
| Millerandage | Vine disorder caused by cold and wet weather at the time of flowering, resulting in some grapes failing to achieve ripeness while others on the same bunch continue to ripen. | None. |

Not all types of disease are bad, however. Some of the most unctuous and ethereal dessert wines are produced from grapes that are infected with a very particular type of rot, *botrytis cinerea*. Unlike other types of rot, this one helps concentrate the sugars inside the grape, but it never punctures the skin and so the juice remains intact. It occurs naturally when conditions are cool and moist in the morning, and eventually give way to warm, sunny, and dry conditions in the afternoons, thereby slowing the growth of the rot. The water in the grape evaporates but the levels of acids and sugars rise. If the weather is too warm and moist for extended periods of time, the fungus will overtake the grapes altogether. This official diagnosis is called gray rot.

Critics use the term "botrytized" to describe these dessert wines that exhibit long lasting sweetness matched with tingling acidity and balance. Due to the residual sugars, many of these wines can age gracefully for years. The most famous wines are made using white grapes and are produced in Sauternes, France, and in various parts of Germany.

*Grapes affected by Millerandage; some berries have matured while others remain small.*

In addition to molds and fungi, insects and moths can be also harmful to the ripe fruit. It is common for insects to find refuge in the grape bunches for nesting purposes. The moist and sugary environment of the inner sanctum of a grape bunch is ideal for larvae growth. Animals such as foxes, rabbits, and squirrels are also problematic during harvest season as the ripe grapes are succulent treats for the critters.

*The most notorious of all pests is* phylloxera, *a tiny aphid that nearly wiped out all of Europe's vineyards. The aphid kills a grapevine by sucking the plant's roots. In the late nineteenth century, as travel between Europe and the Unites States became increasingly easier, growers in Europe grew anxious to experiment with vine species native to America. As a result, American vines were transported back to Europe in high frequency, bringing with them* phylloxera *and thereby causing panic of epic proportions. Although the pest left the American vines alone, it swiftly destroyed established vineyards across the continent. Since there were no symptoms of grape damage or leaf discoloration that were commonly associated with other vine diseases, growers could do nothing but scratch their heads.*

*After nearly all remedies were explored and all resources exhausted, growers finally figured out that native American vine species were immune to the aphid. By grafting European vines onto American roots, the aphid was rendered powerless.*

*Because* phylloxera *often fails to infiltrate vines at high altitudes, areas such as the European Alps, New Zealand's Southern Alps, and Chile's Andean vineyards need not worry as much about this particular disease.*

# What's Up with Global Warming? Is It Affecting Wine?

As mentioned earlier, the ideal growing areas for grapevines are between certain latitudes where the temperatures provide sustainable vine growth. If the temperatures throughout the world increase evenly, this will push the limits of vine production outward from the equator. There are a few different results that will play out, each laced with positives and negatives.

First, it is a boon to areas at the cooler end of the limits, and enables the possibility of making quality wines. We've already begun to see more plantings and more quality winemaking occur in areas like southern England.

Logic would have it that areas teetering with too much heat today will be *too* hot in twenty years, but global warming regarding wine production isn't a zero-sum game. Winemakers have learned how to battle rising temperatures, and although the harvest season seems to be commencing at an earlier pace year after year, advances in science still enable winemakers to grow grapes and produce wine. Such measures include superior nutrient-enriched irrigation practices and acidification (adding acids to crushed grapes that are too high in sugars) prior to fermentation. Critics deem some of these practices as doctoring the wines and that the final products are "produced in a lab," but rarely are these acidified wines noticeable compared to wines that are not. Either way, there is enough momentum and innovation in agriculture to keep these troubled areas producing wines for some time.

Growers can also modify the vineyards and change the grapes and species they grow. The limits of which grapes can grow where are constantly being tested. Change will come slowly to many of the premier winemaking areas in Europe, where the rules for wine production are very implicit about which varieties can go into the wines bearing that designation.

Despite the growing dialogue of increasing temperatures, many winemakers seem unfazed. After all, working with what nature provides is at the core of their habits, and making adjustments is instinctual.

# What Does It Mean When Wine Is Organic, Sustainable, or Biodynamic?

There's a lot of discussion about organic wines and sustainable farming in the world of wine. A big problem is that there is no international standard for what constitutes organic, sustainable, and biodynamic farming. The European Union has one set of regulations; the United States has its own interpretation, and so on and so forth. The lack of an international regulating system can create confusion for the consumer, but the main principles of each are outlined here.

*Winemaker Gunther di Giovanna walking through rows of fava adjacent to his vineyards. The beans impart nitrogen into the soil.*

## Organic

Organic farming is defined by the removal of chemicals and employing the use of natural elements in their place. Manure is used for fertilizer. Cover crops are grown sporadically throughout the vineyard to add nutrients to the soil. Natural sprays such as sulfur are used to control fungal diseases and rot. One of the more interesting features of organic farming is Integrated Pest Management (IPM). This area of science involves the in-depth knowledge of the lifecycles of insects and pests and aims to use pesticides in the most judicious and careful application so as to have a minimal effect on the environment, animals, and humans, and property.

While many winemakers practice organic methods, only a small percentage of these properties can claim "organic" on their wine labels if they haven't passed the requirements set forth by their governing country or region. In most cases, the properties must pass a series of tests over the course of a few years to receive certification. These lengthy procedures and intense monitoring ensures that growers who want to advocate their philosophies are truthfully doing so. In the United States, the Department of Agriculture oversees farming practices, and wineries that market their wines "made from organically grown grapes" must adhere to the rules outlined by the National Organic Program.

It should be noted that many small organic vineyards in close proximity to nonorganic farms aren't likely to ever achieve organic certification. The chemical composition of a piece land is partially defined by what occurs in the surrounding hills, rivers, lakes, and the direction of the wind. If a neighboring farmer who grows cabbage and lettuce uses chemicals in his or her fields, it is near impossible for the grape grower across the road to prove to a governing body that none of those prescribed chemicals ends up in the soil of the vineyards. To this end, many small properties that practice organic grape growing will never bother to apply for certification.

## Sustainable

The choices made by sustainable farms revolve around the efficiency of the resources needed to operate, focusing on the environment, economic profitability, and human and social equity. This includes recycling initiatives, energy and water conservation, the elimination of fossil fuels, and employee benefits, among others. Usually, there is an emphasis on organic vineyard practices, but not always.

Sustainable farms reserve the right to use pesticides and chemicals, but only reactively and when necessary, not according to a preventative or prescribed schedule. Sustainability goes beyond the unit level of a winery. The level of social responsibility of all those that the product touches, such as laborers, policymakers, shippers and distributors, retailers, and the end user collectively measures the impact and success of sustainability. Due to its vast interpretation, there is no accredited body governing what constitutes sustainable or not. Wine labels that read "made from sustainable farmed grapes" or "naturally farmed" are generally meaningless in the legal scope.

*Wine made from organically grown grapes in Sambuca di Sicilia, Sicily.*

## Biodynamic

Perhaps the most unique of all three genres, this type of farming is based on the teachings of Austrian scientist Rudolph Steiner. He believed that farming is an agricultural act that is rooted in a connectedness to the land around us, the energy of the earth, and a relationship with the cosmos. While he believed in the principles of organic farming, Steiner stated that biodynamic goes further and suggested certain vineyard practices should be conducted in accordance with the changing of the seasons and zodiacal calendar. The teaching are extensive, and many winemakers who practice biodynamic may not follow all the steps prescribed, but they generally believe that there is a symmetrical bond between the soil of the earth and the crops we grow with those of gravity, lunar cycles, and astrological influence.

Most biodynamic vineyards practice organic and also include some measures of sustainability; after all, an underlying rule of biodynamic farming is that a grapevine is a living, breathing, and sustainable entity in the universe. To be certified biodynamic, a grower must meet the requirements set forth by the global organization Demeter, named after the Greek goddess of the harvest. Based in Germany, this organization has more than forty certifying chapters located throughout the world.

These categories of organic, sustainable, and biodynamic farming can be difficult to navigate, especially due to the fact that there's no governing body to oversee the processes and labeling. The most important thing to remember is that farming that benefits the long-term is good for everyone. Wine expert Tom Stevenson sums it up best in his authoritative book *The Sotheby's Wine Encyclopedia*: "It should be pointed out that many good growers, and all the best, are 'almost' organic the world over, since anyone who is interested in producing the best wine they possibly can will realize that it is in their own interest to ensure that their own viticulture is sustainable for the long term."

# Winemaking Process

All wine is made from grape juice that goes through a process called alcoholic fermentation. The methodology differs slightly for sparkling, white, red, and dessert wines, but fundamentally they all begin as grape juice. After ripe grapes are picked from the vine, they are brought to the winery and crushed to make grape juice. Yeast is added to convert the sugar (fructose) into alcohol and carbon dioxide. The fermentation process is a simple reaction that has occurred naturally in nature for thousands of years, but due to breakthroughs in science and the human desire to test the limits of wine production, the modern process of making wine has become a bit complicated. At its core though, it is a very simple procedure. The chemical reaction is represented below.

$$Sugar + Yeast \longrightarrow Alcohol + Carbon\ Dioxide$$

As sugar is transferred into alcohol, heat is produced. It is important to control the temperature of fermenting juice so that the yeast cells can continue working efficiently. If the temperature rises too high, the yeast cells become less effective and more volatile, which results in residual sugars and off-putting flavors and aromas. In most cases, the fermentation tanks are equipped with refrigeration capabilities. Otherwise the tanks are stored well below the ground and subterranean temperatures provide the proper conditions. Fermentation usually occurs in stainless steel vats, but sometimes producers use cement talks, glass tanks, or wood barrels.

Carbon dioxide is another by-product of fermentation. If the gas is released, the finished wine will be a still wine; if the carbon dioxide is retained, the finished wine will be sparkling.

*Stainless steel tanks in Calabria, Italy.*

# Where Does a Wine's Color Come from?

Winemakers measure the sugar levels in the grapes throughout the summer. Once the grapes are ripe, they are cut from the vine and brought to the winery for immediate pressing. If the fresh grape juice macerates with the skins, the juice will take on the color of the skins. The longer the juice and the skins remain in contact, the more color the wine will take on.

Most white grapes are crushed with barely any skin contact, and the finished wines are clear and white to off-white. There are some white wines that are made from macerating the skins with the juice before fermentation, and these wines usually take on colors of deep yellow, crimson, and even orange, depending upon the actual color of the grape. White grape varieties such as Pinot Grigio actually have grayish and copper-toned skins.

Oak barrels also add color. Although the influence is less noticeable in red wines, the golden raisin color of white wines is usually a result of aging in oak barrels. As the wine rests, the wine takes on the color (and also the flavor and tannin) of the wood.

Did you know white wine can be made from black-skinned grapes? When crushing the grapes, the

*Harvest workers manually crushing Montepulciano grapes in Abruzzo, Italy.*

juice is separated immediately from the skins. The resulting wines are sometimes referred to as *blanc de noir*, which translates to "white from black."

## *What is yeast all about?*

Native yeasts cling to grapes naturally. Some purists ferment their wine using only these yeasts, believing they allow the grape to fully express itself. However, native yeasts typically take a long time to ferment and they sometimes don't convert all the sugar into alcohol. For this reason, many winemakers prefer to use cultured yeasts, which are widely believed to give winemakers more control.

The fermentation process lasts anywhere from one to six weeks, and in some cases can take much longer due to the types of yeast used, the temperature during fermentation, and the vessel in which the fermentation takes place. There are only trace amounts of residual sugar in the wine following fermentation. Even though a wine may taste fruity or sweet, those are the flavors of the grape expressing itself, and not necessarily actual sugar. The variety of flavors of different grapes is what makes wine drinking very exciting. Sure, fruitiness is a desirable quality in a wine, but it should kept in check by other qualities such as acidity, tannin, and alcohol.

## What are sulfites?

Sulfites are preservatives widely used in winemaking. When sulfur dioxide—chemically similar to sulfite—is added to fermenting wine, the sulfur kills any remaining yeast cells that have yet to transfer the sugar into alcohol. This method allows winemakers to control the alcohol content of the finished wine. Yeast cells also create small amounts of sulfur during fermentation. Following fermentation, the remaining sulfites act as a preservative for the finished wine. This helps to prevent volatility in the wine throughout its life as it journeys around the world before being consumed.

## Are sulfites dangerous?

It is debatable whether or not heightened levels of sulfites are hazardous to your health. To date no substantial evidence of damaging effects exists, but some people certainly have lower thresholds for sulfites. Many wine specialists recommend having something in your stomach when consuming wine. This will aid in digestion and the absorption of sulfites and the other components of wine.

## What is malolactic fermentation?

All reds and some white wines undergo a second fermentation. In this case, bacteria are used to transfer the malic acid into lactic acid. When malic acid is dominant, the wine is bright, crisp, and sharp. After malolactic fermentation, the new lactic acid gives the wines softer, rounder, and creamier complexions. The process also creates diacetyl, a compound that gives off the aromas of heated butter and cream. It is a process that's commonly used to make white wines taste soft and creamy, without the use of expensive oak barrels.

*White wines from Burgundy are some of the best white wines produced in the world, due in part to their aging capabilities. In the 1990s, producers began using less sulfites with an eye towards more "natural" wines. Some of these wines are showing signs of oxidation as they reach 15 to 20 years of age, whereas in the past, white Burgundian wines were know for aging twice as long. Professionals feel that the reduction of sulfites during this time period is to blame for these oxidative qualities, helping to drive momentum back in favor of heavy-handed sulfur treatments.*

# How Are Wood Barrels Used in the Winemaking Process?

*Top-of-the-line barrels from a reputable cooperage can cost as much as $1,000.*

After fermentation, the wine is transferred to a different vessel for maturing. In a process called racking, hoses and tubes move the wine from the fermentation vat to another vessel. In most cases, this next vessel is either a stainless steel tank or a wood barrel. If the wine is placed into an oak barrel, the flavors and tannin in the wood blend with the flavors of the wine, adding depth and complexity. If the wine is placed into stainless steel vats, cement tanks, or any other "neutral" vessel, the finished wine is a truer expression of the grapes themselves.

*Small French oak barrique barrels in the cellar of Casa E. di Mirafiore in Serralunga d'Alba, Italy.*

*Large Slavonian oak barrels in the cellar of Giacomo Borgogno e Figli, in Barolo, Italy.*

Numerous factors determine the final effect the barrel has on the wine. The most important are the origin and type of the wood, the amount of time the wood was dried, and the intensity of the char (fire) when heating the wood to bend the staves into form. Oak is the leading choice, but there are other types of wood used, including chestnut and cherry. Barrels from certain countries tend to offer specific flavors. For instance, French barrels often give the wine flavors of vanilla, cream, toast, and caramel. American oak is preferred for winemakers seeking flavors of dill and coconut (common in Spanish wines).

The size of the barrel is equally important. A small barrel will have a stronger effect on the finished wine than a larger barrel will, due to the greater ratio of surface area contact in small barrels. There are many different sizes of barrels, but the most common size is barrique, 225-liter capacity (about 300 bottles, equal to 60 gallons). This size is used throughout Bordeaux and Burgundy, and the success of these wine regions has made barriques the standard for most other appellations. However, not all wines are aged in these small barrels. Some producers still prefer larger casks, claiming small barrels are too influential on the final wine.

The age of the barrel and whether it has been used before for wine storage are also important. New barrels are stronger than old barrels, which have been stripped of their flavor. Winemakers use terms like *first passage* and *second passage* to refer to the first time and second time that that a barrel was used to mature wine, respectively. After the third use, barrels are deemed "neutral." By this time, previous wines have extracted all the charred flavors and nuances from the wood.

Wood barrels provide trace amounts of oxygen into the wine. As wine ages in oak barrels, there are small amounts that evaporate through the staves. Allowing oxygen into the equation may seem fallible, but slow and controlled oxidation gives the wines beautiful aromas.

*An Australian worker scrapes the sides of the barrel to reinvigorate. the lees, or dead yeast cells.*

## How are wines filtered?

After maturation, the wine is again racked to another vessel for filtration. This involves adding compounds such as bentonite to the wine, which attract any dead yeast cells or leftover debris. Most wines are filtered, but not always. Some critics of filtration claim that the wine is "stripped" of its identity when filtered before bottling, but nonetheless it is quite common.

*Whistler Tree, appropriately named for the numerous species of songbirds that occupy its branches, was planted in Portugal in 1783 and is the oldest known cork tree. The 2000 harvest of bark supplied enough cork for 100,000 bottles of wine, more cork than most trees supply in a lifetime.*

# Bottling and Shipping

Finally the wine is bottled and ready for consumption. The traditional glass bottle, usually 750 ml, is the most popular format, but other options include kegs, bag-in-box formats, and plastic and cardboard packages, all of which are generally viewed as eco-friendly alternatives.

Cork, the most popular closure for wine, dates back hundreds of years. Cork trees must grow unadulterated for twenty-five years to form enough bark to be harvested. Then it takes about ten years to regenerate enough bark for every additional harvest. Most cork trees are planted in the Mediterranean basin, growing prominently in Portugal, Spain, France, Italy, and Northern Africa. Each wine cork has cell membranes impermeable to gasses and liquids. Extremely flexible, they provide an airtight closure for wine.

In the past fifty years, cork has come under fire for the increase of off-flavors and undesirable aromas in wine. As wine production boomed during the latter half of the last century, cork producers upped production as well. As they increased supply, the overall quality of corks declined, and a growing portion of wines were turned away due to cork taint. Cork taint is caused from 2-4-6 trichloroanisole (TCA), a chemical compound that gives undesirable aromas and flavors to wine.

As the proportion of "corked" wines rose, wineries asked cork producers about alternatives but were given few options, or much in the way of compassion. As a result, screw caps, plastics and synthetics, and other types of closures have made their way into the marketplace. Bottling equipment is extremely expensive to replace, so if a winery chooses to change its closures, it is usually a well thought-out and drastic change to the landscape. There are pros and cons to each type, and the jury's still out on which closure is best. Wine professionals view screw caps and other alternatives as effective, if not better, in the short term, as cork. Nevertheless corks are still the standard for wines intended for considerable aging.

## What are some by-products of wine?

Brandy, grappa, and marc are made by distillation, the process of boiling a liquid, trapping the alcohol-rich vapors and steam that rise up, and then cooling the vapor back to liquid. Brandy uses distilled wine, while grappa and marc come from distilled pomace (the leftover skins, seeds, and pits from the winemaking process). The most famous grape brandies in the world are Cognac and Armagnac from southern France, but all winemaking countries produce brandy in some capacity. Since grappa and marc are made from a combination of solids and liquids, they are sometimes more astringent, resulting from the tannin in the components of the grapes. There are many high quality grappas and brandies to be found, many of them aged in oak barrels for considerable lengths of time, resulting in complex and elegant flavors. They're best enjoyed after a meal to aid in digestion.

*A wine cork is composed of 500 million polyhedral (14-sided) cells.*

*Of the tens of billions of bottles of wine, more than 70 percent have cork closures.*

# What Are the Different Types of Wine Produced?

*A wall-mounted display illustrates the effects of a bottle of sparkling wine as it undergoes secondary fermentation in the cellar of Cantine Ferrari in Trento, Italy.*

*Bottles going through the riddling process in the cellar of Cantine Ferrari in Trento, Italy.*

## Sparkling Wine

Chardonnay and Pinot Noir are the main grapes used in sparkling wines. Chardonnay provides the finesse and flavor, while Pinot Noir lends structure and backbone. Indigenous grapes are also used in their respective countries.

As previously mentioned, trapping the carbon dioxide created during fermentation produces sparkling wine. Two methods are used almost exclusively: the Champagne Method and the Charmat Method.

## Champagne Method

The Champagne Method is the more important of the two processes. A number of base still wines are combined to achieve a desired blend. (The term *cuvée* is sometimes used to denote a superior quality of the blend using only the finest base wines, but there is no international standard.) Once the blend is determined, the new wine is placed into the bottle. A small dose of yeast and sugar is added and finally the wine is sealed with a crown cap (similar to a beer bottle cap). The combination of sugar and yeast is called the *liqueur de tirage*. A secondary fermentation then occurs directly in the bottle. As the added juice and yeast interact, the carbon dioxide integrates with the flavor of the wine and the dead yeast cells fall to the bottom of the bottle. Since the bottle is capped, the carbon dioxide is retained in the liquid. The exposed contact with dead yeast cells also provides a creamy and rich flavor. The longer the exposure, the richer the finished product will be (and usually more expensive).

Over time the bottles are rotated and eventually are standing upside down so that the spent yeast cells fall to the neck of the bottle and rest on the under surface of the crown cap. This process of rotating the bottles methodically over the course of long period of time (usually more than a year) is called "riddling."

Next, the neck of the bottle is exposed to cold temperatures to solidify the sediment. The bottles are turned upright and the crown cap is removed. Upon opening, the pressure inside the bottle expels the sediment out, leaving behind the clean and almost-finished sparkling wine.

Finally, a second addition of reserve wine is added to top off the wine. The varying levels of sugar in this last step will determine the overall level of sweetness in the sparkling wine, if any.

Then, the cork is added and the wine is closed with a wire cage to secure the cork.

The Champagne method is a trademarked name, so it is illegal for any producer outside of Champagne, France, to use the term on a bottle. Rather, producers list "Classic Method," "Traditional Method," or "Bottle-Fermented" to refer to this style of sparkling wine production. While expensive and time consuming, it is unarguably the best way to produce premium bubblers.

## Charmat Method (Tank Method)

In the Charmat Method, the secondary fermentation is done in large tanks and then the finished wines are bottled afterwards. A more economical method, it is generally used to make wines meant for immediate consumption. Prosecco is the most popular wine made in this fashion.

Critics refer to the carbonation in sparkling wines as "the bead." The carbonation resulting from bottle-fermentation is usually softer and well integrated with the wine, whereas the Charmat method produces wines with slightly coarser bubbles.

*Due to the labor- and grape-intensive processes, and consumers' unremitting preferences for still wines, for every ten bottles of wine produced in the world, only two are sparkling.*

*Below is a list of the various styles of sparkling wine in increasing levels of sweetness.*

*Extra Brut*
*Brut*
*Extra Sec*
*Sec*
*Demi-Sec*
*Doux*

*Sediment from secondary fermentation after the neck of the bottle was exposed to freezing temperatures to solidify the sediment.*

# Vintage and Non-Vintage Wines

*Producers make vintage-labeled sparkling wines about three years in every ten.*

Some sparkling wines list a vintage, or year, in which the grapes were grown; others simply say "NV," which stands for "non-vintage." The former must be made using grapes from only the year listed. This implies that the growing season was exceptional and the grapes were superior to other years. Vintage sparkling wines are not made every year, only in the years where the winemaker feels the grapes are ideal. It goes without saying the majority of producers within a given region all produce vintage wines in the best years and none of them make vintage wines in poor years. Vintage wines are aged much longer during the secondary fermentation than are non-vintage wines. Some vintage sparkling wines are intended for aging. As they get older, the carbonation subsides and the flavors and aromas grow stronger, more complex, and more ethereal. Some of the most expensive and collectable wines in the world are vintage Champagne.

Non-vintage wines are made using base wines from different years. Some producers use dozens of base wines from varying vineyards and even different years. This is done to reproduce the same tasting wine year in and year out, creating a "house-style," a taste that a consumer can rely upon with every purchase.

Many sparkling wine houses produce both vintage and non-vintage wines. The non-vintage sparklers are consumed as everyday drinking wines, while the vintage bottles serve as premium age-worthy wines.

## White Wines

The main difference between white wines and all other wines is the minimal skin contact during the maceration process. In most cases, white grapes are pressed and the juice is separated from the skins, seeds, and stems after just a few hours, if not immediately. Studies show that crushing the grapes and keeping the juice cool throughout the fermentation process helps maximize the aromatics of the grapes. During fermentation, winemakers can stir the lees, or dead yeast cells. This process adds richness to the wine through the extraction of glycerol. It is also done generously to white wines fermenting in wood barrels to limit the extraction of color and pigment of the wood barrels into the wine.

Small quantities of white wines are made from red grapes with the skins immediately separated from the juice after the grapes are pressed. White wines from Pinot Noir are used in the blending stages of sparkling wine production prior to secondary fermentation.

## Rosé Wines

Rose wines are made by one of two ways. Winemakers can either blend white wines and red wines to achieve a desired color and taste or they can bleed off juice from macerating black grapes. The remaining juice is kept on the skins and is used to make red wines. From the French word *saigner* (to bleed), the process of bleeding off pink juice is known as *saignéer* and is considered the better of the two ways to produce pink wine. Rosé wines are highly seasonal and best enjoyed during the summer months. They're pleasant because they have the fruitiness of red wines combined with the crisp and fresh profile of white wines.

## Red Wines

The color pigments in the skin give red wine its color. The longer the juice macerates with the crushed skins, the more color the wine takes on. It is a slippery slope though, because the wine will also take on tannin from the skins, seeds, and stems. Overly tannic wines taste bitter and astringent and are seen as a winemaking flaw. Just the right balance of color and tannin will yield wines of both beauty and strength.

## Dessert Wines

Most dessert wines are made using dried grapes. Sometimes winemakers leave the grapes on the vine well into the fall or they're picked and brought to the winery to dry. As the grape begins to shrivel, the sugar levels rise and water evaporates, resulting in concentrated sugar levels. Crushing and fermentation commence as normal, but winemakers will stop the fermentation at some point to preserve the natural sugars in the wine. Some dessert wines can age for decades, as the sugar acts as a preservative.

## Fortified Wines

The Arabs were the first to discover distillation in the eleventh century. It would be another 600 years before distillates were added to wine. Thankfully, we are blessed with many types of fortified wines today. The most famous are port, sherry, Madeira, and Marsala. Neutral-grape spirits (odorless and tasteless distilled wine) are added to either fermenting wine (in the case of port) or to recently fermented wine (in the case of sherry). In both cases, the alcohol suspends the yeast cells and any residual sugar remains in the wine. In the end, the excess sugar and alcohol help preserve the wine, making fortified wines some of the most age-worthy. There are many vintage Madeiras and ports from the 1800s still being consumed today. Vermouth is another type of fortified wine made from grapes. It is usually aromatized with herbs and other flavorings and used as a mixing agent for cocktails.

# Part Three

## Enjoying Wine

While understanding how wine is made—
and appreciating the effort, science,
intuition, and patience that goes into
producing one bottle—is certainly valuable,
it is equally important to just relax and
enjoy the wine that is in your glass at any
given moment. There will certainly be
wines that you dislike, but keep tasting
and trying wines from new regions and
produced from grapes you've never
heard of. You will quickly learn about
your own preferences as you delve
deeper into the world of wine.

# Evaluating Wine

Below is a step-by-step guide to evaluating wine.

## Sight

A wine's appearance can tell you more than you think. Young wines are usually more monotone than older wines. White wines range from straw yellow to green to slightly opaque. Red wines run the gamut from bright cherry to dark purple and garnet. Wine color is determined by grape variety, the length of time (if any) the juice and skins macerate prior to fermentation, the type of fermentation vessel, and the type of maturation vessel (if any). As wines age, however, these colors change in the bottle as the pigments break down. White wines take on darker yellow colors and eventually yield to brown. Red wines take on colors of crimson, brick, and eventually brown.

Some terms used to describe a wine's appearance: light, opaque, brilliant, browning, cloudy, dirty, hazy, inky.

## Swirl

Swirling the wine in the glass helps aerate the wine. When interacting with oxygen, the wine releases its aromas and aldehydes. No need to vigorously swirl the wine; a gentle swoosh will help the wine release what's hiding within. It is best not to pour the wine up to the brim, thereby ruining any chance of swirling. Rather, fill the wine up to no more than halfway to the top; this will enable you to swirl freely.

Be careful with sparkling wines. While it is okay to swirl a bit to release some aromas, over-swirling can cause the wine to go flat and lose its signature carbonation.

## Smell

The first sniff won't make or break the experience, but it is a good way to get a glimpse at what's in there. Inhale and think about what jumps out at you first. Fruitiness? Earthiness? Alcohol? Are there aromas that you've smelled before? Some grapes, such as Syrah or Grenache, have a vast array of aromas, depending upon the winemaker and the region where it is from. Other grapes, such as Sauvignon Blanc or Muscat, show similar aromas despite where and by whom they're crafted. Identifying these patterns helps establish a solid memory base of grape profiles. Once you've analyzed the first smell, go in for a second dive. By now the first smell should have eliminated any residual aromas in the air that were trapped inside your nostrils. This second sniff should be clearer, and you'll be able to build upon your first impressions.

Some terms used to describe a wine's smell: earthy, woody, nutty, herbaceous, fruity, spicy, floral, vegetal, chocolate, savory, mineral, animal.

## Sip

This is the stage where we further build upon our thoughts from smelling the wine. Does the wine taste like it smells? Does it smell like it tastes? What is most obvious about the taste? Is it the fruit? Is there an oaky or wood component?

Acidity has been mentioned a few times throughout this book, but here is where it plays its most important role. Acidity is the most crucial and least credited aspect of a great wine. Acidity is the tingling sensation in the back of your cheeks, and this is the component of wine, especially whites and sparkling wines, that helps break down food particles and gives wine its unique food applicability. It also keeps a wine in check over the life of the aging process, and the best older wines in the world still have a zippy, balanced flavor. Wines are called "flabby," "fat," or "dead" when the acidity is either non-existent or overwhelmingly drowned out by higher levels of sugar, fruitiness, tannin, or alcohol.

Some terms used to describe a wine's taste: astringent, approachable, austere, balanced, big, bitter, bright, chewy, closed, creamy, crisp, delicate, developed, dry, earthy, elegant, fat, flabby, flat, fleshy, fresh, green, hard, herbal, hot, light, long, maderized, mature, meaty, metallic, moldy, nutty, oaky, off, oxidized, rich, seductive, short, soft, stalky, sulfuric, tannic, tart, thin, tired, toasty, woody, yeasty, young.

## Slurp

As you taste the wine, breathe in through your mouth, forcing air over your tongue and maximizing exposure to the olfactory bulb in the back of your throat. This is the main sensor that sends signals to your brain, determining whether you like or dislike what you're tasting. By breathing in, you maximize the exposure of the wine to the back of your throat.

## Savor

The final step is to continue enjoying the wine while admiring its transformation, as it never ceases to evolve in the glass. As long as it is exposed to oxygen, the wine will change accordingly.

*The streaks that form on the side of a wineglass, trickling down and retreating back into the wine, are described as a wine's legs. Some people mistakenly think that legs are a sign of quality, believing the larger and more robust the legs, the better the quality of the wine. Not true. The legs of a wine are an indication of its alcohol content. Light and subtle legs indicate the wine is low in alcohol, while heavier and more viscous legs suggest higher alcohol content.*

*Feel free to move the glass around your nose and take in every corner of the glass because each nostril can detect different smells. There may be a lot to process; in 2004, two Nobel Prize winning scientists determined that there are more than 10,000 different aromas we can detect.*

*An unofficial seventh step, spitting, is a common sight at formal wine tastings. Since the throat has neither taste buds nor flavor receptacles, there is no need to swallow the wine.*

# Flawed Wine

There are two reasons you may dislike a wine:

1. Unappealing taste, aroma (subjective)
2. The wine is flawed and does not taste the way it was intended by the winemaker (fundamental)

The first reason is rather common, as there are plenty of wines out there that are unsuitable to your tastes, but there are also a number of reasons a wine will taste different from what the winemaker intended. In this case, the wine is called "flawed" or "off." These problems occur during the winemaking process or somewhere along the distribution process. They are isolated to a very small proportion of the wine produced, less than 10 percent, but they still occur.

Below is a list of the main signs of flawed wines:

| Smell/Taste | Reason |
|---|---|
| Vinegar, sherry | Oxidation - prolonged exposure to oxygen/air |
| Nutty, caramel, brown, rancid | Maderized – usually exposed to light and/or heat during transportation |
| Dank, wet-mold, musty | Faulty corks (referred to as a "corked" wine) |
| Burnt matches, gaseous | Too much sulfur dioxide used in the winemaking process |

Having an awareness of flawed wines helps you differentiate between the reasons you dislike the wine. If you simply don't like the taste, you know to steer clear. If the wine is fundamentally flawed, you shouldn't be discouraged to try another bottle of the same wine.

If you encounter any of the above kinds of defects, return the wine to its source. Simply put, if you're in a restaurant, inform the manager or sommelier that you believe the wine is spoiled. Same goes for a wine shop. Most reputable wine shops will exchange a flawed bottle for a new one.

The problem of "corked" wine is troubling because there is no visual indication prior to bottling that a particular cork will result in cork taint. Therefore, we currently have no way of determining whether the wine is "corked" until we've purchased and opened the bottle.

## How can I train my palate without buying and tasting wine?

Since the flavors and aromas of wine are found in nature, it is easy to practice without actually tasting wine.

Begin training your palate for the main components of wine: acidity, tannin, sugar, and fruit.

Acidity–lemon juice. Concentrate on where in your mouth you feel acidity. It should be felt largely in the back of your mouth at the base of your cheeks, but in this kind of concentrated dose, you'll probably feel it all over your mouth.

Tannin–over-steeped tea. Found in grape skins, stems, and seeds, as well as in oak barrels, tannin helps provide structure and power. Sometimes the tannin is overwhelming; other times it is barely noticeable. Usually we feel tannin between our cheeks and gums.

Sugar, Fruit, and Other–mixed fruit, chopped up strawberries, blackberries, bananas, lemons, herbs, spices, flowers, oak chips. Chop up the fruit or herbs and place them into a wineglass with a little bit of water. Sniff each glass to smell its aroma.

# Keeping a Wine-Tasting Journal

Remember what you've tasted and your reactions by keeping a detailed journal. Many of the world's esteemed wine critics and personalities have extensive records of tasting notes of wines they liked and disliked.

Below are three entries for the same bottle of wine. Each entry represents a different skill set and comfort level with wine. None is better than the others, although specificity leads to deeper and more precise evaluations. But there's nothing wrong with beginner-level descriptions. If that's the extent of how you like to analyze wine, then so be it. Never forget, enjoying wine is the underlying purpose of consuming it.

## All three tasters jot down the following information:

Producer: Castle Rock Winery

Grape(s): Pinot Noir

Vintage: 2009

Appellation: Carneros

Country: USA

Price: $13.00

Tasting Date: October 19, 2012

Then they move on to tasting and evaluating the wine.

## Beginner Level

Color: Purple

Aroma: Fruity, earthy

Taste: Plum, jammy, smooth

Finish: Medium

I think this would pair well with: Mom's roast beef

Because: I like the taste of both of them on their own, so they'd probably pair well.

## Intermediate Level

Color:  Light to medium-bodied, purple and violet

Aroma:  Mix of plums and earth, with slightly oaky notes

Taste:  Balanced acidity and fruit. Blackberry and plum are most prominent, with subtle notes of toast. Firm tannin, yet not too abrasive.

Finish:  Medium, not too long, but silky and smooth

I think this would pair well with:  Mom's roast beef

Because: The wine isn't too intense so it won't overpower the flavor and texture of the meat. It also has a fruity element that should pair well with the sweetness of the marinara sauce.

## Advanced Level

Color:  Light to medium purple with garnet hues and crimson edges.  Legs are medium to form and medium to fall, indicating a moderate alcohol content. Wine is just above opaque and is very clear; no noticeable sediment.

Aroma:  Soft and pleasant with cooked plum aromas and complex toastiness. Herbal notes of fresh vegetables, mushrooms, forest floor, and clove.  Reminiscent of Old World Pinot Noir, but more robust and fruity.

Taste:  Initial burst of blackberry fruits with toffee notes. Smooth and clean with moderate tannin and balanced acidity. Fleshy, yet not too astringent. Secondary flavors of graphite and chalk show through after the fruit dissipates. Flavors of bitter chocolate are prominent on the back palate.

Finish:  Slightly chewy and long with lasting flavors of spicy fruits and peppery notes.

I think this would pair well with: Mom's roast beef

Because: The wine isn't too big and gripping for the roast beef, but it has enough structure and tannin to cut through the fats and proteins. The wine has a great spice and clove note which could pair well with the herbs and spices already in the meat. The fruity components of the wine will pair nicely with the sweetness of the marinara sauce.


*Your skills will develop over time, but with each entry try to be more precise in your description. In no time, you'll be writing wine reviews for the local paper!*

# Pairing Food and Wine

Just as consumers disagree about which wines are pleasurable on their own, there will always be debates and disagreements about which wines to pair with certain foods. The most common rule is: "white with fish, red with meat." While I don't think this is bad advice, it isn't very complex.

## Similar Flavors, Contrasting Flavors

One place to start when pairing food and wine is to identify similar flavors that they share. BBQ ribs and brisket practically cry out for a big, smoky, and peppery red. A creamy, oaky white compliments a creamy seafood dish.

Another option is to focus on wines that contrast the flavors on the plate. A crisp white is a great choice for soft cheeses. The firm acidity and bracing minerality helps clean the palate of all the gooey-ness and richness of the cheeses and prepares you for your next bite.

Always consider the weight of the food and the weight of the wine. Pair salads, mild cheeses, crackers, appetizers, and other light foods with light wines, regardless of whether the wine is sparkling, white, red, or dessert. A heavier wine could overpower the flavor and delicacy of lighter foods, such as sushi or caviar.

The following guide outlines the main principles of wine's various characteristics and how they're relevant to food.

**Acidity** *Great with tart foods and lighter dishes. Acidity cuts through a wide array of flavors and textures.*

**Tannin** *Ideal with heavier dishes, especially meat proteins. Also great with bitter flavors and pretty much anything grilled or charred. Be careful with tannic reds and fish courses. Tannin and fish oil can lead to metallic and displeasing flavors. Steer clear of spicy foods and tannic wines. Tannin accentuates the heat in the dish, so for heavily seasoned dishes stick to lighter and softer wines.*

**Sweetness** *Sugary unctuousness moderates heat and spicy dishes as well as saltiness. It also complements sweetness and takes the edge of foods high in acidity.*

**Oak** *Oak generally gives wines a heavier complexion. Pair oaked wines with foods that are grilled, smoked, caramelized, charred, or broiled to match the bitterness found in the wine.*

**Alcohol** *Higher alcohol wines, whether white or red, can feel heavier, denser, and richer in the mouth. Pair lower alcohol wines with lighter dishes and higher alcohol wines with heavier, richer fare.*

*The creamy, rich flavors of cheese are perfect compliments to the tannin and acidity in wine.*

# Regionality

If it grows together, it goes together. Pairing wines with foods from the same region is an easy rule to follow. Since the grapes and the food were both exposed to the same soil, climate, and atmosphere, it is logical to assume they share similar qualities and intensities. For instance, cheese and wines of the same region can be perfect companions. The clean acidity of Sancerre, a French white wine, is perfect to wash away the creamy tang of Cherignol, a soft goat milk cheese that comes from the same area. In Italy, Parmeggiano-Reggiano is produced from cow's milk and must be aged for a long period of time. The cheese is crumbly, salty, and powerful. Lambrusco is a unique red wine from the same area. It is classified as *frizzante*, meaning slightly sparkling. When paired with the cheese, the unctuous red fruit flavors of the wine add sweetness to the dry and crumbly texture of the cheese, and the gentle effervescence of the wine helps clean the palate—cutting through the saltiness. Should you ever venture to either of these areas, you're sure to find these wines and cheeses paired together in copious amounts.

## What are some classic food and wine pairings?

Most food and wine books touch upon a few classics that are great springboards for finding your own perfect pairings. When you see why they work, you can channel that energy en route to creating your own memorable pairings.

**Champagne and Caviar.** Champagne is the unequivocal sparkling wine. The gelatinous, mouth-popping saltiness of the caviar is gently washed away by the effervescence of champagne, but not before the biscuity, yeasty, and citrus flavors of the wine add their own touch, creating extremely long, salivating sensations.

***Recommended Champagne:***
Taittinger Brut Prestige NV  $
Larmandier - Bernier Blanc de Blancs Extra Brut 1er Cru NV $$
Krug Grand Cuvee Brut MV  $$$

**Chablis and Oysters.** Fresh oysters are cold, creamy, tangy, and rich. Just as wine connoisseurs nitpick the differences between wines, the oyster cognoscenti can wax poetic all day about the provenance of oysters. Chablis is the unmistakable pinnacle of crispy, steely, flinty, and racy Chardonnay. Many of the vineyards grow in clay and chalk soil, resting on a subsoil of maritime deposits. The resulting wines often have a saline component to them, ideal for the briny flavors and fleshy texture of oysters. There's no better way to begin a meal than with a half dozen beausoleil oysters and a glass of Chablis. In the words of wine writer Jay McInerney, "If you've never had oysters with Chablis, you should rectify this failure immediately."

***Recommended Chablis:***
Jean-Claude Bessin Vieilles Vignes $
Domaine Faiveley 1er Cru Fourchaume $$
Pascal Bouchard Grand Cru Blanchot $$$

**Barolo and White Truffles.** Truffles grow in the roots of trees, and the most famous truffles hail from Italy and France. Members of the tuber family, they exude decadence and intoxicating aromas when thinly sliced. Barolo is deemed "the king of wines and the wine of kings," and its growing region is one of Italy's most important red wine appellations, producing powerful and age-worthy wines from the indigenous grape Nebbiolo. In Italy, the marriage of fresh white truffles and Barolo is almost worth taking out a second mortgage on your house. The ethereal aromas of white truffles from Alba are matched only by intense earthy and mushroom flavors and scents of Barolo. The combination is truly a regal experience.

*Recommended Barolo:*
Mirafiore  $
Borgogno $$
Giuseppe Rinaldi Cannubi $$$

**Sauternes and Fois Gras.** Fois gras is produced from duck or goose liver. The practice of raising and over-feeding ducks for the production of fois gras has come under intense debate, but it is still a culinary delicacy and is one of the extreme delicacies of gastronomy. The best fois gras preparations have a gamey tenderness with a buttery and creamy texture. Sauternes is the most famous dessert wine, produced in southern France. The unctuous lemon and honey flavors of the wine blend well with the flavors of fois gras, yet the cloying acidity of the dessert wine helps clean the palate from the gelatinous trail left behind by the fois.

*Recommended Sauternes:*
Château d'Arche $
Château Rieussec $$
Château d'Yquem $$$

## Cooking with Wine

Wine adds a touch of acidity to any dish being prepared. The alcohol in the wine is cooked off and the flavors dissipate, so don't worry too much about which wine to use for your culinary needs. Just make sure that the wine you select is something you'd also drink. There isn't much point in cooking with a wine that you wouldn't sip on its own.

*Aggravating "A" Foods:*

*Asparagus – Methionine, an amino acid found in asparagus, makes wines taste metallic or vegetal. If you can't live without asparagus, stick to light wines, especially whites. Grilling asparagus also minimizes the effects of methionine.*

*Artichokes – Cynarin, a compound found in artichokes, causes wine to taste sweet or sometimes dull and closed. Stick to high acid wines produced from Sauvignon Blanc or Sangiovese. You can also try white dessert wines.*

# Understanding Wine Labels

Navigating a label is one of the more challenging aspects of mastering wine, turning some people off wine altogether. Luckily there are a few constants for all wine labels that are required by law, especially those imported into the United States.

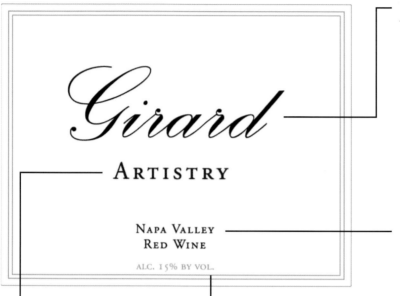

**Name of the Producer or Winery** One of the most important aspects to a wine label, it signifies which company produced the wine. Producers sometimes list contact information, website addresses, and even scannable codes on the back of the label in smaller font.

**Appellation or Growing Region** Signifies where the grapes were grown before being pressed to make wine. Learning which appellations you like is helpful in finding your way in the world of wine because most appellations have rules regarding which grapes can be used and how the wine is made. When they exist, these rules ultimately have an effect on the finished product and tend to create somewhat similar, yet discernibly unique products.

**Brand Name of the Wine** A brand name can be the name of a vineyard, the name of a relative, dialect for anything of particular significance of the wine, and pretty much anything and everything in between. It can also simply be the name as the winery itself. It is also referred to as the proprietary name or fantasy name. Anything is possible for brand names, unless they're misleading to the consumer or infringe upon other brands by other producers.

**Alcohol Content** Indicates the alcohol content in the wine. Most dry wines contain between 8 and 17 percent, but dessert wines and fortified wines range anywhere between 5 and 25 percent. While it is helpful to the consumer to know the strength of the wine, this information is also necessary for customs because higher tariffs are placed on higher alcohol wines. Most countries permit an allowance of +/- 1 percent or so.

**Grape(s) Used to Make the Wine** This vital piece of information (not required, but commonly listed when available) helps consumers choose wines based on grapes they're familiar with. In many of the U.S. appellations there are allowances for adding other grapes to a wine in small quantities, yet still labeled with only the dominant grape variety. For example, a winery in California can produce a wine based on Cabernet Sauvignon and add up to 15 or 20 percent of other varieties such as Merlot, Syrah, etc. The wine can still be labeled Cabernet Sauvignon, and there's no obligation to disclose the other grapes. In Australia, however, blended wines must state all the grapes used and list them in descending order. Since the rules vary from place to place, do some homework before you buy.

**Vintage in Which the Wine was Produced** The year when the grapes were grown and produced into wine. Weather conditions are never the same year after year, so your favorite wine will change with each vintage. In some cases the changes will be minimal and unnoticeable. Other times a wine will change drastically from one year to the next. Vintage charts and reports that rate each year are important for those who collect wines, since great vintages generally produce age-worthy wines, and it is helpful to know when wines are worth buying and cellaring or worth buying and consuming.

2007

BRUNELLO DI MONTALCINO
DENOMINAZIONE DI ORIGINE CONTROLLATA E GARANTITA

GOVERNMENT WARNING: (1) ACCORDING TO THE SURGEON GENERAL, WOMEN SHOULD NOT DRINK ALCOHOLIC BEVERAGES DURING PREGNANCY BECAUSE OF THE RISK OF BIRTH DEFECTS. (2) CONSUMPTION OF ALCOHOLIC BEVERAGES IMPAIRS YOUR ABILITY TO DRIVE A CAR OR OPERATE MACHINERY, AND MAY CAUSE HEALTH PROBLEMS.

CONTAINS SULFITES

RED WINE - 750 ML - ALC. 14% BY VOL.- PRODUCT OF ITALY
BOTTLED BY: SAN POLO S.A.A R.L. MONTALCINO-ITALIA

LEONARDO LOCASCIO SELECTIONS

IMPORTED BY:
WINEBOW INC.,
NEW YORK, NY.

7 48789 70402 2

**Country of Origin** States the country where the wine was produced.

**Name of the Importer** Wines are imported by licensed companies that handle logistics, storage, and customs procedures. In some cases the importer also acts as the sole distributor of the wines and markets the products to retail wine shops and restaurants. In other cases the importer sells to a licensed distributor, which then sells to other outlets. Contacting the importer is always a great place to start when tracking down a specific wine. Similar to producers, importers often give website addresses and other contact information, and are very welcoming to inquiries. If the wine is domestic, there is no importer. The next time you're enjoy a great wine at a friend's party, take note of not only the brand name, but also the importer.

*Girard*

SAUVIGNON BLANC
NAPA VALLEY

OUR SAUVIGNON BLANC IS FERMENTED IN STAINLESS STEEL TO MAINTAIN BRIGHT, CRISP FLAVORS THAT ACCENTUATE THE RIPNESS AND FULLNESS THAT WE ACHIEVE FROM PICKING OUR GRAPES LATER IN THE SEASON. RICH CITRUS AND GREEN APPLE FLAVORS ARE ABUNDANT. MADE WITH NATIVE YEASTS AND NO MALALACTIC FERMENTATION, THIS WINE IS RICH IN FLAVOR WITH A REFRESHINGLY SMOOTH FINISH.

FOR INFORMATION OR TO JOIN OUR WINE CLUB
707-968-9297
GIRARDWINERY.COM
VISIT OUR TASTING ROOM AT
6795 WASHINGTON STREET IN YOUNTVILLE, CA

CONTAINS SULFITES     750 ML     ALC. 13.9% BY VOL.

GOVERNMENT WARNING: (1) ACCORDING TO THE SURGEON GENERAL, WOMEN SHOULD NOT DRINK ALCOHOLIC BEVERAGES DURING PREGNANCY BECAUSE OF THE RISK OF BIRTH DEFECTS. (2) CONSUMPTION OF ALCOHOLIC BEVERAGES IMPAIRS YOUR ABILITY TO DRIVE A CAR OR OPERATE MACHINERY, AND MAY CAUSE HEALTH PROBLEMS.

PRODUCED & BOTTLED BY GIRARD WINERY, HEALDSBURG, CA

0 08176 70040 3

**Volume of the Bottle's Contents** Indicates how much wine is inside the bottle. The standard bottle is 750 ml, or three quarters of a liter. This equates to roughly 25 ounces. Winemakers use a wide variety of bottle sizes and shapes to bottle their wines, so it is important to have the actual volume listed on the label. Sometimes the volume is etched into the glass itself.

### *Girard*

#### ARTISTRY
#### NAPA VALLEY RED WINE

ARTISTRY IS OUR PROPRIETARY BLEND OF 59% CABERNET SAUVIGNON, 19% CABERNET FRANC, 5% PETIT VERDOT, 11% MALBEC AND 6% MERLOT. OUR GRAPES COME PRIMARILY FROM BOTH HILLSIDE & VALLEY FLOOR VINEYARDS IN OAKVILLE & ST. HELENA. RICHLY TEXTURED & ELEGANTLY BALANCED WITH FORWARD FRUIT & INTEGRATED TANNINS.

For information or to join our wine club 707-968-9297 girardwinery.com
Visit our Tasting Room at 6795 Washington Street in Yountville, CA

CONTAINS SULFITES  750ML  ALC. 15% BY VOL.
PRODUCED & BOTTLED BY
GIRARD WINERY, SONOMA, CA

GOVERNMENT WARNING: (1) ACCORDING TO THE SURGEON GENERAL, WOMEN SHOULD NOT DRINK ALCOHOLIC BEVERAGES DURING PREGNANCY BECAUSE OF THE RISK OF BIRTH DEFECTS. (2) CONSUMPTION OF ALCOHOLIC BEVERAGES IMPAIRS YOUR ABILITY TO DRIVE A CAR OR OPERATE MACHINERY, AND MAY CAUSE HEALTH PROBLEMS.

**Sulfite Advisory** All wines imported into the U.S. must be treated with sulfites to serve as a preservative and stabilizer. The level of sulfites can differ greatly from one wine to the next, but the minimum for all wines imported must be around 10 ppm (10 parts per million). Sulfur dioxide is usually added to the wine to arrest fermentation.

**Government Warning** All wines (or any beverage with more than 0.5 percent alcohol) must state the health effects of consumption, including birth defects, impaired ability to operate machinery, and general health problems.

*The standard volume of a wine bottle is 750 ml (25 ounces). This came about during the late 1800s when glassblowing became a more common trade. Glass bottles for wines were often structured and blown with the capacity of one long exhale. Since peoples' lung capacities varied, the sizes of the bottles varied, but on average each single breath would produce a bottle of about three quarters of a liter, and thus was born the standard size bottle.*

# Decanting

Decanting is the process of pouring the contents of a wine bottle into another receptacle—usually an ornate decanter made of glass, but not always.

There are two primary reasons to decant wine.

As wines age, they develop sediment. This is a byproduct of the components of the wine (tannin, acidity, and others) breaking down. Sediment is an odorless and tasteless component of old wines, and it is always a good sign to see sediment when opening an old bottle of wine. Decanting helps to separate the wine from the sediment.

Decanting quickens the time for wine to breathe. Age-worthy wines are loaded with tannin and acidity, and the rapid exposure to air helps mitigate the "chewy" and "astringent" character of these young wines.

A third but no less essential reason for decanting is the pure joy of serving and enjoying wine from something other than the bottle. If you don't finish the wine, pour it back into the original bottle, rather than leaving the remainder in the decanter. You want to minimize the exposure to air.

## Can decanting be harmful to a wine?

Absolutely. Some wines, if too old, quickly lose their aromas and flavors if "shocked" with too much oxygen. The longer a wine ages in the bottle, the more fragile it becomes. Decanting old wines that cannot sustain the rush of oxygen can result in lost flavors and sadly, lost enjoyment. There's no solid rule of thumb, but you should proceed with caution with any wine more than 30 years old.

It should be noted that decanting is done infrequently in Europe. There is a special kind of joy that results from pouring half glasses or small tastes of wine into a glass repeatedly until the wine is gone. With each new small pour, there are new aromas and flavors to enjoy as the wine has been decanting inside the bottle. The more oxygen (and less wine) inside the bottle, the more effective the oxygen is.

*Quite a few products are available that help aerate wine without the use of a decanter. Many of them are large spouts or plastic devices that fit into the top of the bottle and then help spread the wine out as it is poured into the glass.*

*Most wine professionals will agree that the wineglass is the best decanter, and swirling wine in the glass helps aerate it the most effectively.*

*Decanting helps aerate wine and releases its aromas and flavors.*

# Aging Wines

Of the 35 billion bottles of wine produced each year, less than 1 percent are intended to age for longer than five years. Most are meant for immediate consumption, within one to five years. The majority of wines exhibit all the things we like about wine in balanced proportions, such as fruit, acidity, earthy or mineral tones, and alcohol. Wines intended for aging, however, are much less enjoyable in their youth. The principle agent responsible for ageability in wine is tannin. In young wines meant for later consumption, the tannin levels are through the roof and mask many of the other desirable qualities we seek in a wine. Although these wines develop much more complex flavors and aromas over time as the tannin and other components of the wine break down, they do so at the expense of immediate enjoyment. The other two components necessary for an age-worthy wine are acidity and alcohol, although the latter typically applies to fortified wines such as Madeira, port, sherry, and Marsala.

We mostly think of red wines (Bordeaux, port, Burgundy, Barolo, Napa Valley Cabernet, Rioja, among others) when discussing age-worthy wines, but there are some white wines made from grapes such as Riesling, Gewurztraminer, Pinot Blanc, and Chardonnay, to name a few, that can age gracefully for decades. Since white grapes generally undergo a shorter maceration time with the skins before fermentation, the key to an age-worthy white wine is acidity, and there are only a handful of white grape varieties with the genetic makeup required for extensive bottle aging.

Alcohol also acts as a preservative. Fortified wines such as sherry, port, Madeira, and Marsala have the added benefit of higher alcohol levels to deflect the off-putting aromas of "over the hill" juice.

As wine ages, it loses the primary flavors of fresh fruits, and takes on *secondary* and *tertiary* flavors. It also loses color. White wines generally take on golden yellow colors and red wines change from ruby red to brick and crimson. Sediment forms. (The lack of any sediment in an old wine is suspicious and could mean the wine is fraudulent.)

# How to Properly Store Wine

You don't need an expensive wine cooling unit or wine fridge to stash a little wine away for a rainy day, but there are a few guidelines to follow.

- Lay corked wines on their sides. This practice prevents the cork from drying out, which would allow oxygen to seep in, expediting oxidation.

- Lay wine bottles with the label facing upwards. This ensures that you can retrieve the bottle, display it to your guests (if any), and open the wine without the sediment going back into the wine.

- Avoid direct sunlight. Never display a wine in a windowsill or on a table where long hours of sunlight can penetrate the glass. Doing so can cause spoilage and emit maderized flavors (nutty, caramel, vinegar-esque). A dark place like a basement or closet is best.

- Find a quiet place where there are little to no vibrations. Underneath the sink or staircase means the wine will be prone to constant motion and vibration, which can affect the quality in the long term.

- Beware of temperatures too hot or too cold and also extreme fluctuations in temperature. If a wine is exposed to a wide range of temperatures throughout the aging process, the lifespan of the wine dramatically decreases, and the wine can spoil.

- Keep in mind the humidity. Persistent humid conditions can cause corks to swell, and then when temperatures fall and the humidity retreats, the corks will retract a bit. Leaky corks are always bad news. If wine can get out, oxygen can get in.

Overall, waiting for wines to age requires patience and care, but the splendors of a properly aged bottle of wine are tough to beat.

If a wine tastes or smells like vinegar, chances are it is past its prime. In such cases the wine is said to have "turned." There's not really much to do except dump the wine or find a culinary application for it. You're still welcome to enjoy the wine as you see fit. I've known many friends and colleagues who

*Laying bottles on their side is crucial, as the cork remains moist and intact. Otherwise it can dry out and crumble, letting in air.*

proudly admit to consuming an old and expensive bottle of wine, even though it was past its peak drinking period. The heartache and lamenting of dumping a bottle of wine can be too much for some of us, understandably so.

## *How long does a bottle of wine last after opening?*

Once a bottle has been opened, oxygen will slowly turn the wine into vinegar. The more air (and less wine) inside the bottle, the quicker the wine will turn. The less air (and more wine) inside the bottle, the slower the effect of oxygen. Regardless, once the cork has been lifted, the clock is ticking. There's nothing wrong with opening a bottle of wine, sipping one glass, and enjoying the rest within a few days. In fact, some bottles of wine may even taste more appealing after a day or two of breathing.

## *What if the wine has a screw cap or another closure other than cork? Does this mean it isn't meant for aging?*

Certainly not! Many producers are switching to screw caps for wines intended for years of cellaring. There are also reports of old wines from the 1970s and 1980s that aged well for decades beneath a screw cap.

*The Coravin Wine Device is a new wine product that incorporates argon gas into a wine bottle through a hypodermic needle, which is inserted through the top of the bottle, piercing the foil capsule and cork. Attached to the device is a canister of argon gas. As the bottle is poured, wine is sent through the needle and is replaced by argon gas from the canister. The wine inside the bottle never comes in contact with the outside environment, which would cause the wine to oxidize and spoil. You can pour a taste, a glass, or most of the bottle, and the remaining wine inside the bottle will keep for months, if not years.*

Some ways of combating oxidized wine is to transfer the leftover wine to a smaller bottle, thereby reducing the ratio of oxygen-to-wine. Ensuring a tight seal, you should re-cork the bottle thoroughly. For sparkling wines, use a sparkling wine stopper, which are easy to purchase at wine shops and gourmet cooking stores. The stoppers have clamps that fasten to the underside of the lip at the neck of the bottle, ensuring an airtight seal that traps in the carbonation. You should avoid sealing a sparkling wine with a cork, for the air will eventually dissipate through the cork and leave the wine flat. The cork is also liable to be expelled from the bottle due to the carbon dioxide trying to escape.

# Are There Benefits to Buying Large Bottles of Wine?

Larger-format bottles age better than regular-sized bottles of wine, the reason being that the air trapped between the wine and the cork has a lesser effect on a larger bottle. The more liquid inside the bottle, the smaller the ratio of air to wine, which results in a slower and more defined development of the wine. Large bottles are also less prone to spoilage when exposed to periodic fluctuations in temperature. Like many things in life, the bigger they are, the more costly they become, and much of the rare and collectable wine trade is made up of larger-format bottles, mostly of French Bordeaux, Champagne, and Burgundy.

The following is the hierarchy of bottle sizes. Many are named after biblical figures. Two different categories for large-format bottles exist, and some names refer to two different sizes.

| Bottle Equivalent | Champagne/Burgundy | Bordeaux |
|---|---|---|
| ¼ bottle (187 ml) | Piccolo | |
| ½ bottle (375 ml) | Half Bottle (Demi) | Half Bottle (Demi) |
| 1 bottle (750 ml) | Standard Bottle | Standard Bottle |
| 2 bottles (1.5 l) | Magnum | Magnum |
| 3 bottles (2.25 l) | - | Marie-Jeanne |
| 4 bottles (3 l) | Jéroboam | Double Magnum |
| 6 bottles (4.5 l) | Réhoboam (discontinued in 1989) | Jéroboam |
| 8 bottles (6 l) | Methuselah | Impériale |
| 12 bottles (9 l) | Salmanazar | Salmanazar |
| 16 bottles (12 l) | Balthazar | Balthazar |
| 20 bottles (15 l) | Nebuchadnezzar | Nebuchadnezzar |
| 24 bottles (18 l) | Melchior | Melchior |
| 26.5 bottles (20 l) | Solomon | - |
| 33 bottles (25 l) | Sovereign | - |
| 36 bottles (27 l) | Primat/Goliath | - |
| 40 bottles (30 l) | Melchizedek | - |

# Does the Shape of the Bottle Matter?

Bottles come in many different sizes, shapes, and colors. It is common to see the same types of bottles used by producers from within certain growing areas, usually due to time-held relationships with glass producers, but at the end of the day, the shape and size have no bearing on the flavor of the wine.

Below and on the facing page are some of the more common types of wine bottles. Most are named after classic Old-World growing appellations, and producers will often choose certain shapes depending upon the grape variety used to form an association with the grapes used in the originating appellation. For instance, a producer who makes wine using Pinot Noir will opt to use the Burgundian-shaped bottle. There are no hard rules to bottling wines, so don't be thrown off if you see discrepancies with the guidelines below.

**Bordeaux** The classic bottle that is straight-sided with steep curving shoulders. The shoulders of the bottle that lead up to the neck are helpful for catching sediment (should there be any) as the wine is poured out. Historically this shape has been used for wines from Bordeaux, France, and also for wines that are made using Cabernet Sauvignon, Zinfandel, and Merlot. Lately though, this bottle has become universal for all kinds of grapes and wines from all over the world.

**Burgundy** Wider and shorter than the Bordeaux bottle, it has longer and gently sloping shoulders. It is famous for wines from Burgundy and the Rhône Valley in France as well as wines made from Chardonnay, Pinot Noir, Syrah, and Grenache from other countries.

**Alsace/Mosel/Rhine** Tall and slender with long, gently sloping shoulders. In the Rhine region of Germany, the glass is usually a dark brown color, whereas in Alsace and the Mosel it is more common to find the wines in green bottles. Elsewhere, it is used to bottle wines made from the same grapes that make the wines from Alsace and Germany famous: Riesling, Pinot Blanc, Pinot Gris (Grigio), Sylvaner, and Gewürztraminer. Rosé wines are also used for this kind of bottle, especially European rosé wines from Southern France.

**Champagne/Sparkling** Thick glass, a long neck, and gently sloping shoulders characterize these bottles that must be strong enough to withstand the pressure inside the bottle. The top lip of the bottle is also much thicker than other bottles, to ensure the wire cage affixed to the top of the bottle will keep the cork nested in place.

**Fortified** Short and fat with rigid shoulders. These bottles are usually smaller than other types of bottles, because fortified and dessert wines are sometimes bottled in 375ml and 500ml sizes. The shoulders are intended to catch sediment that forms after years in the bottle, a common occurrence with vintage ports and Madeiras.

*The weight of the glass alone contributes to 40 percent of the total weight of a bottle of wine. Due to high shipping costs, many producers and countries are exploring alternative packaging options, such as plastics, kegs/barrels, and cardboard.*

## Does the color of the glass matter?

Glass color is important only when discussing wines intended for aging. Clear or green glass bottles offer little to no protection from sunlight, which over time can break down some of the more desirable antioxidants in a wine, causing spoilage and oxidation. Wine bottles using clear or green glass are usually intended for immediate consumption. Most, if not all, wines intended for aging are bottled using dark brown glass.

## What is the indentation on the underside of the bottle?

The "punt," sometimes referred to as the "kick-up" or "dimple," gives the wine bottle stability and lowers the chances of it falling over. It is also helpful for pouring wines by providing a grip for the thumb. A punt also helps collect sediment at the bottom of a bottle. As sediment forms over time, it settles on the bottom of the bottle and is distributed to the outer edge, forming a thick ring. The indentation makes it less likely for the sediment to be redistributed back into the wine when the bottle is finally served.

## What is the capsule on the top of the bottle for?

The foil capsule helps keep the edge of the cork clean and serves as a decorative element. It is sometimes emblazoned with a brand logo or some other image of the winery. Capsules were once produced from lead, but it was widely believed that residue from the lead capsules remained on the glass rim of the bottle and leeched into the wine as it was poured out. Most capsules are now made from some form of tin or aluminum, or a combination of the two.

## Does the shape or size of the wineglass matter?

A wide range of glasses today caters to certain styles of wine and even certain grape varieties. Riedel, Bormioli, and Spiegelau are some of the major suppliers of beautiful stemware lines of different sizes and shapes. While it is nice to have a set of glasses for your Pinot Grigio wines and another set for your Riesling wines, it is not necessary.

So while many different wineglasses are available, the two most important aspects are a wide bulb (middle of the glass) and a narrow rim (top of the glass). This ensures that the glass will collect the aromas in the space above the wine's surface and travel up the glass. The wineglass should also be large enough to allow ample swirling. Look for glasses anywhere between 8 and 15 ounces (250 to 450 ml).

Sparkling wines should always be served in flutes. A thinner and elongated wineglass helps maintain the delicate carbonation that makes bubbly what it is. If this sparkling wine is served from a wide glass, the effervescence will dissipate quicker.

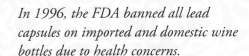

*In 1996, the FDA banned all lead capsules on imported and domestic wine bottles due to health concerns.*

*The shapes and sizes of glasses vary, but to get started you only need one or two glasses.*

*A corkscrew is the main device used to remove the cork from a bottle of wine. There are many styles and versions of corkscrews, but they all have the vital components needed for opening a bottle, most importantly the worm and a handle for leverage.*

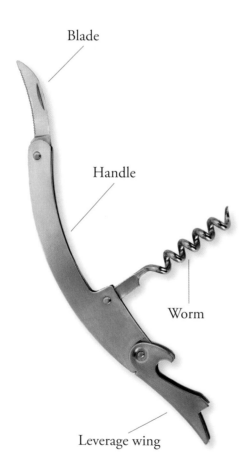

Blade

Handle

Worm

Leverage wing

## What is the correct way to open a bottle of sparkling wine?

Opening a bottle of bubbly can be dangerous if you're not careful. Follow these steps to ensure not only safety, but also so you don't end up wasting some of the wine or losing the precious carbonation.

1. Remove the top of the foil capsule. Usually there is a tab or string, sometimes referred to as a "zipper," at the base of the wire cage meant for easily removing the foil.

2. Unwind the wire cage that surrounds the cork by placing your thumb on the top of the bottle with one hand and unwinding the wire with your index finger and thumb on your other hand. At this point, you never want to take your thumb off the top of the bottle. Leave the wire cage on the cork but loosen it on all sides.

3. Grip the bottle with the palm of one hand, while keeping your thumb on top of the wire cage with the other.

4. Slowly rotate the bottom of the bottle while gently wiggling the cork out of the top of the bottle. By keeping the wire cage on at all times, you can use it to help get a good grip on the bottle.

5. You'll feel the cork easing out of the bottle, which gets easier and quicker as more of the cork is exposed.

6. When finally removing the entire cork, try to do it slowly so the wine barely makes any sound or hissing noise, which is the sound of carbon dioxide leaving the bottle. The louder it is, the more gas is released. Since you want to retain as much of the gas as possible, the less noise the bottle makes the better.

Note: Unless you're winning the World Series of baseball or the Daytona 500, you absolutely do not want to shake the bottle. This will cause the wine to shoot out of the bottle immediately after the cork is removed. While celebratory in nature, you'll end with less wine to enjoy, and the wine left inside the bottle will go flat quickly.

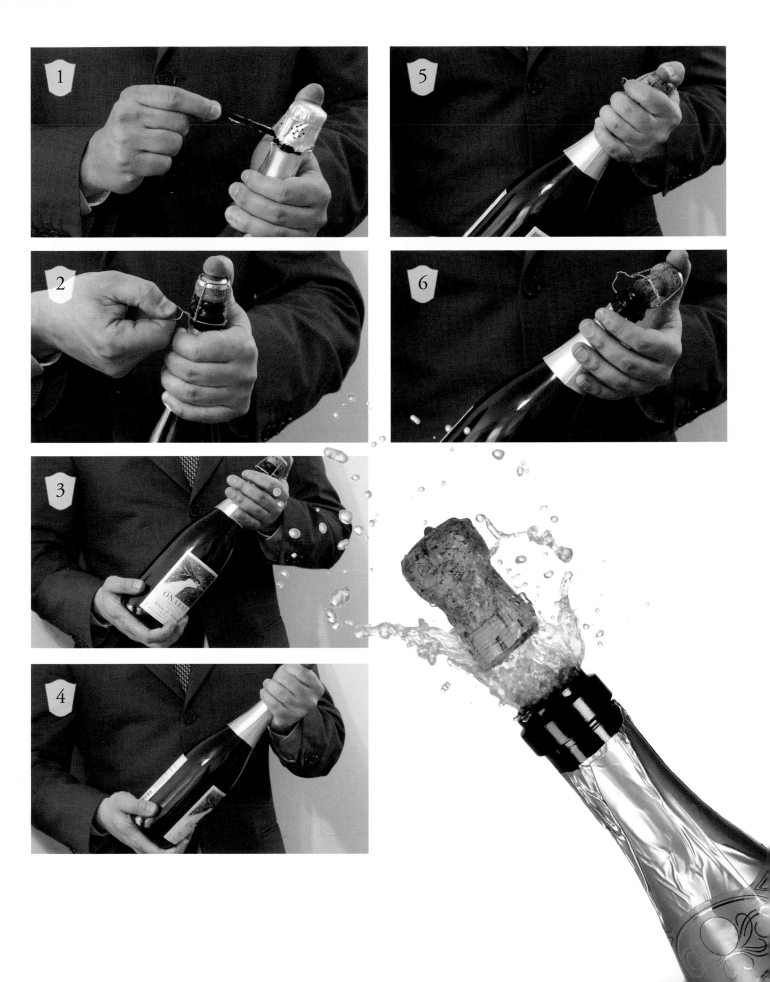

# Host Your Own Wine-Tasting Party

Now that you're enjoying and learning more about wine, why not share your new interest with friends and family by hosting a wine-tasting party? But before you do, follow these steps to ensure your event goes smoothly.

## *Choose the format.*

Consider what you'll serve. Are you aiming for just a wine tasting or more of a social food/wine event? Is it a formal sit-down or a casual mingling with friends? The answers will dictate the wines you serve and how you serve them.

Pairing regional foods and wines is a good place to begin your wine-hosting career. Whether it is a sit-down dinner or finger foods and nibbles, throughout the evening pair the food and wines that are typically served together in the host country. For example, a well-rounded Spanish food and wine event may look something like this:

**Cataluña**
Tomato-rubbed bread with ham
Casteller - Cava Brut

**Galicia**
Octopus with Potatoes
Bodegas Santiago Ruiz - Rías Biaxas

**Castilla y Leon**
Roast Lamb and Garlic Soup
Telmo Rodríguez – Ribera del Duero, "Gazur"

**Andalucía**
Flan de Café
Emilio Lustau – Pedro Ximénez Sherry, "San Emilio"

*Be sure to have on hand a bowl for dumping wine. Inevitably there will be guests and wines that disagree. Encouraging them to finish their glass without the option of dumping is improper etiquette. It is also important to have water readily available.*

If you want to focus more on the wine, aim for areas that are known for a wide variety of styles. For a California tasting, a nice spread would be six wines: one red and one white from the southern, central, and northern appellations. Or you can focus only on Napa Valley, taking three wines from the valley floor appellations and three from the mountain appellations. Another option is to do a U.S. tasting and serve wines from New York, Oregon, Washington, and California.

A different way to go is to offer five or six (or more) wines that are made using one specific grape variety. Syrah, Cabernet Sauvignon, Riesling, Chardonnay, and Sauvignon Blanc are grown all over the world, and the wines they produce are widely available, and usually starkly different in color and body. If it is the summertime and white wine is on everyone's mind, try throwing a Riesling-themed event with one Riesling wine each from Australia, Argentina, California, France, Austria, and Germany. You can evaluate the similarities and differences en route to the ultimate wine experience.

### Choose the stemware.

You can have one glass for each wine per person. It is not necessary but it helps in a more formal setting. For a more casual approach, use just one glass per guest and encourage tasters to re-use their glass. As discussed before, the sizes and shapes of the glasses shouldn't be a major headache for you, but if you have different sets of glasses, try to use the wider-bowled glasses for the more aromatic wines to showcase the bouquets.

### Decide the order of serving.

Some people opt to have all the wines available right from the start, while others like to control the pace and the wines being served. If you're going to taste the wines one at a time, start light and build up to the heavier wines. It is optional to provide any kind of write-up or literature about the wines, but guests appreciate it because there are usually a few in the bunch who are shy about asking questions in front of others.

Here are some different kinds of wine tastings to try at your next get-together:

**Vertical Tasting** Tasting different vintages of the same wine in sequential order, usually from youngest to oldest. This is a great exercise to understand the benefits of the aging process. (Example—tasting the 1990, 1995, 1998, 2000, and 2004 vintages of Elvio Cogno's Barolo, Ravera)

**Horizontal Tasting** Tasting different wines of the same vintage, usually from the same region. This is a fun exercise as it shows how different producers make stylistically unique wines although the grapes are grown within a small zone. (Example–tasting red Burgundy wines from the 2005 vintage only from the Côte de Nuits.)

**Blind Tasting** While challenging, this kind of wine tasting can be the most exciting as it involves evaluating the wine on its merits without knowing the origin or the grape. All too often, knowing where the wine is from and by whom it is made can influence our opinions. In a blind tasting, we practice how to decipher the regional traits of wines.

# Buying Strategies

Understanding how to analyze wine and pair it with food is certainly a major part of the wine experience, but selecting and purchasing wine is of equal importance (and can bring equal frustration).

The distribution system of alcohol varies from state to state; however, most states use a three-tier system. Wineries sell to licensed distributors, which sell to retail stores and restaurants. Some distributors only conduct business in one state, while others have national distribution channels and large sales forces. Wineries evaluate these traits and seek out companies that will best represent their wines. Smaller wineries and smaller distributors tend to go hand in hand. This is principally why you can sometimes find wine on a business trip to Michigan, but cannot purchase the same wine in your home state of Illinois, simply because the winery's products are not distributed in the latter. If you're lucky, you may be able to buy the wine online.

The ways wines are sold to consumers also vary from state to state. For example, in New Jersey you can purchase beer, wine, and liquor all together within the same building, along with your groceries. Other states, like New York and Pennsylvania, isolate wine and liquor from grocery stores. It all depends upon the state you're in. There are also laws about buying wine in one state and shipping it to another. Some states permit it, while others are adamantly opposed to it.

## *Using the importer and/or distributor*

One of the more common questions I'm asked is: "I just had a great bottle of wine at a restaurant, but where can I find it near my home?" The secret to tracking down your favorite wine is looking on the back of the label for information about the importer or distributor. In most cases, these companies list contact information complete with address, phone number, and website. These websites offer a bevy of information regarding the producer and the different wines produced, and in some cases they offer the names of retail stores and restaurants where you can purchase the wine.

**Importer** This bottle of Italian white wine is imported by Dark Star Imports, located in New York.

## Retail

Most retail wine shops organize their wine by country. This means you'll find all the French wine in one part of the store, all the Italian selections in another part, and all domestic wines in a different location. This makes it easy to target the kind of wine you'd like based on where it originates: a good thing if you're focusing on learning the different appellations of individual countries. This system can be disadvantageous if, for example, you like Sauvignon Blanc and are looking to explore all the different wines from this grape that the store offers. You'll have to walk through all the aisles of all the different countries/states and examine the different wines based on the grape. If you're in a hurry, it is a burden. However if you've got time, strolling the aisles of a great wine shop can be enjoyable, and educational to boot.

Lately, some retailers have bucked the trend and organize their stores according to flavor profile. In one part to the store, you'll find wines that are "lean and crisp," and in another wines deemed "rich and full," while in yet another "big and bold." This can be helpful if you're looking for a certain style of wine. Keep in mind that the wines are chosen and labeled by the wine shop employees; your tastes may different from theirs, and what you deem "rich and full" may very well be "light and soft" to them. Furthermore, it may take you some time to find that bottle of Chianti that you're hoping to score, as you'll have to explore the different shelves unsure if it is labeled "light and dry" or "fruity and fun."

# Buying for Now or Later

Collecting wine isn't the easiest hobby on the pocketbook, but if you're in the market for collecting, it is important to do some research and evaluate which wines are worthy of cellaring for a few years (or decades) and which are intended for immediate consumption. Remember, only a fraction of the wine produced each year is meant for aging longer than five years. Magazines and online editorials have information about the main wine-growing regions all over the world and offer insights into which wines are worth holding and which are worth drinking after purchase.

Experienced wine collectors sometimes buy a case of wine and periodically (about once a year) open a bottle from that case. If the wine is too young (too tannic, bitter, astringent, gripping, etc.), then the others in the case still need time to age. On the other hand, if the wine is drinking beautifully and is enjoyable, it is time to move the case of wine to the front of the line and enjoy the remaining bottles in the coming months and years.

The best advice I can give is to frequent the same few shops for all your purchases. Get to know the wine shop staff on a first-name basis. Talk about wines you like or dislike, wines you've had with great meals, and so on. Sharing experiences helps the staff identify which kinds of wines you like, and will open you up to new varieties from new countries based on your preferences. A convivial relationship with your local shop will keep you abreast of the happenings in the world of wine.

## Restaurants

Similar to retail shops, wines in restaurants are usually listed geographically or stylistically, depending upon the number of selections, type of restaurant, and preferences of the beverage manager. Within this framework, wines are then often listed alphabetically, in ascending price, or progressive in body. A progressive list is one where the wines are arranged from light bodied to full-bodied. Some restaurants offer "suggested pairings" or "sommelier picks," and other categories to further help the customer. In most cases, the wine lists in restaurants are meant to enhance the meal, offering different styles of wine to the cuisine offered. There are, however, restaurants where the wine list takes center stage. These restaurants offer thousands of different selections, many of them rare and older wines, meant to give another experience to the drinker. If the wine list is extremely lengthy, a table of contents is sometimes offered in the beginning.

## The role of the sommelier

Some restaurants are staffed with a wine department with trained sommeliers, or wine stewards, to aid customers with all beverage needs. If you frequent the same restaurants, get to know these passionate wine professionals on a personal level. They're exposed to winemakers and are in the know about the trends in the industry. The team is responsible for sourcing the wines, training the staff, organizing the wine cellar, and helping customers with wine selections during service hours. Asking them for recommendations with your meal is usually a sure way to find what you're seeking.

## The Internet

In 2005, the U.S. Supreme Court ruled that out-of-state wineries and retailers can sell wines via the Internet; however, each state still has autonomy over its own alcohol sales. Some states, mostly those with conservative and older liquor laws, still prohibit all consumer-direct wine shipments. There are currently numerous appeals to the law and the future is uncertain as to the mass adoption of this ruling. Due to its ambiguities, large retailers like Amazon.com are in limbo about entering the wine distribution business. So far, the largest effects seen with online commerce are websites that don't necessarily sell the wine directly to consumers; instead, they connect the consumer and winery. In doing so, they take a small fee of the sale and pass off the liabilities of shipping the wine to the customer.

## The role of the wine critic

Critics and wine reviews have an incredible impact on the wine industry. The 100-point system of rating wines (50-100; 50 being poor, 100 being exceptional) has helped change the landscape of wine buying. Generally, wines receiving high scores outsell those that don't.

There are many benefits to assigning numeric values to wines based on their merits. Wine professionals and critics have extensive tasting notes and strong memory banks, which help intricately describe wines to potential consumers. Keep in mind that the flavor descriptions are very subjective, and a critic's threshold for bitterness, acidity, tannin, and flavors most likely differs from yours. What they like overall, may very well be the antithesis of a good wine to you.

This concept of "higher score, more popularity" has, in turn, prompted some producers to make wines that are geared more towards the preferences of influential critics. Seems like a smart idea, but when a winery changes its mentality so dramatically that the wines are seen as a foreign and clear deviation from what the public generally is expecting based on previous vintages, the winery is scorned for pandering to a global taste. Consequently, the wines fall from favor, and the role of the wine critic is demonized. Those who favor wines of terroir and identity are the loudest critics of this strategy. They feel that a wine should speak of the place it is made, and not be fabricated into a wine that will be assigned a number based on the tastes of one individual with a knack for poetic and superfluous prose.

There is undoubtedly an upside to wine critics. Quality, however it is defined, has made its way down the wine supply chain and the quality of wine at most price levels is much higher. Consumers as a whole are benefiting from the opinions of wine critics.

*Purchasing and cellaring wine is more economical than purchasing the same wine at a later date. As time progresses, vintage wines become costlier. If you are in the market for a wine that you would like to age, compare prices between wine shops and restaurants, since most lists are posted online. After some shopping around, you can usually find a good deal. A rare wine that's limited in production may not be as easy to locate. In that case, inform your local wine merchant and he or she should be able to track it down for you.*

---

*Every seven out of ten bottles of wine purchased in retail stores are consumed within three hours.*

## Part Four

---

# Wines of the World

More than 60 countries produce upwards of 35 billion bottles of wine each year. That's a lot of juice. While the majority produces wine in small quantities, France, Italy, and Spain collectively are responsible for more than half of the global supply. Even though some countries contribute little, what they add is usually quite interesting and the quality is improving as producers adopt new techniques, technology, and equipment.

# Old World Versus New World Wines

The great divide in the world of wine is Old World versus New World. Old World refers to European countries such as France, Italy, and Spain, where winemaking is rooted in centuries of tradition. New World is basically everything else, regardless that wines have been produced in some of these countries, such as Australia and Argentina, for a long time.

A second component to Old versus New refers to how a wine is made and how it tastes. Old World European wines are less fruity, drier, and lower in alcohol, while New World wines are fruity, juicy, high-alcohol, and plump. Of course, this is a simple generalization. Producers in New World countries make wines that are light in color, low alcohol, dry, and rustic. Similarly, some producers in Europe churn out inky, fruity, alcoholic wines.

## Classified Growing Areas

Each country has its own rules about wine labeling legislation, but they're all rooted in the principle of confining zones to geographic boundaries. Within these zones are a variety of rules about which grapes can be grown, alcohol content, yield requirements, and aging requirements, to name a few. Not all appellations enforce each and every category, but the basic premise is this: If you purchase wine called "Napa Valley Cabernet Sauvignon 2012," you're guaranteed that the wine's grapes were grown in the Napa Valley, is based largely on the grape Cabernet Sauvignon, and is produced mostly from grapes grown in 2012. These rules, albeit a bit archaic, protect the producers within these areas and protect us as consumers.

The major criteria that are defined by appellations are:

- Geographical Area
- Alcohol Levels
- Grape Varieties and Blending Guidelines
- Yield Restrictions
- Vineyard Training Methods
- Winemaking Methods
- Aging Requirements

France was the first country to institute a national registry, doing so in the 1930s. Since then many countries have followed suit. Below are the major categories and names of appellation systems for some of the world's leading wine countries:

| United States | American Viticultural Area – (AVA) |
|---|---|
| France | Indication Géographique Protégée – (IGP)<br><br>Appellation d'Origine Protégée – (AOP) |
| Italy | Indicazione Geografica Tipica - (IGT)<br><br>Denominazione d'Origine Controllata  - (DOC)<br><br>Denominazione d'Origine Controllata e Garantita – (DOCG) |
| Spain | Denominación de Origen – (DO)<br><br>Denominación de Origen Calificada – (DOCa) |
| Portugal | Denominação de Origem – (DO)<br><br>Denominação de Origem Controlada – (DOC) |
| Germany | Qualitätswein bestimmter Anbaugebiete – (QbA)<br><br>Qualitätswein mit Prädikat – (QmP) |
| Australia | Geographic Indicator – (GI) |

## Single Vineyard Wines

Many wines are marketed and sold as limited items because they're made from single vineyard grapes. In France the finest vineyards are called Grand Cru and Premier Cru, and these vineyards are specific sub-zones of the appellations in which they're grown. The United States is only just beginning to recognize certain vineyards, and very few American Viticultural Areas are devoted strictly to one vineyard.

Because fruit from one vineyard is much more representative and expressive of the grape, single vineyard wines are usually more expensive than those made from grapes from a wider area. Some vineyards can be ridiculously large, though, defeating the primary purpose of distinguishing it in the first place.

# Old World White Wines

## France

### *Chablis*

The gold standard for white wines is Burgundy, France. Crafted mostly from Chardonnay, wines from this appellation in eastern France age gracefully for decades and are essential to any reputable wine collection.

The Burgundy appellation is a long stretch of valleys and mountains in the east of France. From Chablis in the north to Lyon in the south, the entire appellation covers about 200 miles (325 km). Between these two points are many small, family-run wineries, each specializing with its own winemaking style. Many Francophiles have devoted their lives, and much of their finances, to a life-long study of this region.

Chablis, one of the most famous areas, is in the northernmost part of Burgundy. Its wines were once known for being ultra-crisp, appley, and steely—the epitome of a young and fresh Chardonnay. Nowadays some producers are making softer and rounder styles, more akin to wines further south in Burgundy, where oak barrels are more popular. Although the Chardonnay grape seems to be grown everywhere in the world, the unique conditions in Chablis are ideal. The area is very cool and the soil is mostly clay with chalk deposits. In extremely cool years, the grapes can fail to fully ripen, but when they do, the results are head and shoulders above the rest of the Chardonnay field.

Most of the wines produced in Chablis are intended for immediate consumption, but a few age well. Many of these age-worthy wines are made using grapes sourced from one of the seven Grand Cru vineyards. These tiny parcels of land are located on the gently sloping northern banks of the Serein River, benefiting from the exposure to the sun and the effects of the nearby lake. While many excellent Chablis wines can be found in the $15 to $30 range, wines produced exclusively from the grand cru vineyards can fetch up to hundreds of dollars.

---

### *French Winemaking Terms*

**Côte/Côteaux:** *slope of a hill; hillside*

**Crémant:** *sparkling wine other than Champagne*

**Cru/Cru Classé:** *classified vineyard*

**Doux:** *sweet*

**Millésime:** *vintage*

**Mise en Bouteille au Château/Domaine:** *estate-bottled at the chateau or winery*

**Sec:** *dry*

**Sélection de Grains Nobles:** *dessert wine made from grapes affected by botrytis cinerea*

**Vendange:** *harvest*

**Vendage Tardive:** *late harvest*

**Vieilles Vignes:** *old vine*

*The seven Grand Cru vineyards of Chablis:*

- *Blanchot*
- *Bougros*
- *Les Clos*
- *Grenouilles*
- *Les Preuses*
- *Valmur*
- *Vaudésir*

*An unofficial eighth vineyard, La Moutonne, is comprised of parcels from both Les Preuses and Vaudésir.*

---

*Although it is only 19 miles (30 km) from Champagne and nearly 60 miles (97 km) from the heart of the Burgundy zone, Chablis is a staple of Burgundian whites and is a shining example of the potential of Chardonnay.*

## Côte d'Or

Southeast of Chablis, the Côte d'Or is home to many of the most famous and expensive Burgundy wines. Translated, the name means "golden slope," a reference to the color of the vineyards in the fall as the leaves change color. The entire area is only about 30 miles (48 km) from north to south and just over 1 mile (1.5 km) wide at its widest point. Within the valley are two sub-regions: the Côte de Nuits and the Côte de Beaune. Both regions produce excellent white and reds, but the former is known more for red using Pinot Noir grapes, while the latter region is the epicenter for white wines.

Similar to Chablis, the climate is cool in this part of Burgundy, ideal for maintaining the critical acid levels in the grapes throughout the year. Because wine is so relevant in this part of the world, the winemaking tradition spans generations. If not making wine, families earn their income farming grapes and selling to wineries. Due to strict French law, vineyards are divided between siblings upon inheritance. Over time, family holdings have become fragmented and extremely tiny in some cases, amounting to no more than a single row of vines in certain spots. This is fortuitous should the vines be located within one of the esteemed Grand Cru vineyards or within some of the slightly less prestigious, yet supreme Premier Cru vineyards. For the very best in Chardonnay, wines from the following Grand Cru vineyards of the Côte de Beaune can cost a pretty penny: Le Montrachet, Bâtard; Montrachet, Bienvenues; Bâtard; Montrachet, Criots; Bâtard; Montrachet; Charlemagne.

## Côte Châlonnaise

The next region further south in Burgundy is less famous than the previous areas, but still produces excellent whites. The vineyards are spread out more, rather than in one long chain of vineyards like in the Côte d'Or. There are five main villages for wine production in the Côte Châlonnaise, two exclusively for white and three for red or white.

- Bouzeron (white only)
- Rully
- Mercurey
- Givry
- Montagny (white only)

## Mâconnais

This part of Burgundy produces the most Chardonnay wines—three times more than all other areas combined. Many of them are easy-going, food-friendly, and affordable. The hub of production is in the southeast in the villages of Pouilly-Fuissé, Pouilly-Loché, Pouily-Vinzelles, St-Véran, and Viré-Clessée. The wines from Pouilly-Fuissé have long been the most recognized wines from Mâconnais and are great stepping-stones for entering the world of white Burgundy.

*Solutre Rock overlooking vineyards in Mâconnais.*

When correctly used, oak barrels can elevate a wine from simple to grand. Winemakers strive for the correct marriage of fruitiness from the grapes and oak tannin. Too little oak, and the wine may lack the complex aromas and flavors that develop over time in the bottle. Too much oak, and the fruit will be completely masked. On a quality level, the producers in Burgundy seem to have more consistency with getting it right year in and year out, benefiting from unique climate and soil conditions as well as generations of experience.

---

Of the eight white wine Grand Cru vineyards of Burgundy, seven are located in the Côte de Beaune, the southern half of the Côte d'Or.

---

Aligoté, the other main white grape variety grown in Burgundy, is mostly used as a blending grape throughout the region. However, in the village of Bouzeron all white wine must be produced entirely from Aligoté. The wines are pleasant and approachable, yet lack the depth and complexity of the white wines made from Chardonnay.

---

Look for these producers of Mâconnais wines:

- Maison Louis Latour
- Château-Fuissé
- Domaine Faiveley

---

The town of Chardonnay is located within Mâconnais, one of the earliest places in France to cultivate the grape variety.

*For the best Alsace white wines, look for wines produced from one of the fifty-one Grand Cru vineyards.*

---

*Try these traditional Alsatian cheeses paired with the region's trademark crisp whites:*

- *Bibalakass*
- *Brouère*
- *Bargkass*
- *Munster or Munster Géromé*

## Alsace

The wines of Alsace in eastern France resemble German wines in many ways. The bottles are long, slender, and green, and the names of the producers as well as the grapes sound German. The region has strong ties to Germany, and the constant reoccupation between France and Germany over the course of history has shaped the modern landscape. The cooler climate results in lean grapes that produce lower-alcohol wines. Riesling, Sylvaner, Gewurztraminer, Muscat, Pinot Blanc, Pinot Gris, Chasselas, and Auxerrois are the most common grapes.

When compared to German wines, Alsatians are usually drier yet riper, meaning they have fruity flavors but are technically dry and lack heavy doses of residual sugar. The finish is steely, flinty, mineral, and crisp. Following World War II, German winemaking forked towards partial fermentation and richer, sweeter wines, while Alsatian wines branched towards full fermentation and drier wines.

Alsace had once been praised as the only French region that labels wines with the grape variety. We're beginning to see this method spread to other regions in France, as well as other regions in Europe, but it is one of the reasons that Alsatian wines have gained a loyal following.

Alsace boasts some of the driest conditions in France due to the Vosges Mountains in the west that absorb much of the rain. This enables growers to leave grapes on the vines well into October and November to make off-dry and sweet wines. Wines labeled Vendange Tardive are picked using late-harvested grapes. The wines aren't always sweet, yet there is usually some residual sugar to offset the higher alcohol and richer profile. Even rarer are wines labeled *Sélection de Grains Nobles*, produced from riper grapes infected with the noble rot *botrytis cinerea*.

Vin d'Alsace
APPELLATION ALSACE CONTRÔLÉE

DIRLER-CADÉ

*Bux*
*Pinot Gris*
2010

White Wine
Alc.14% by vol.

750 ml

CONTAINS SULFITES    L 09640

Mis en bouteille à la propriété par
DIRLER-CADÉ EARL VITICULTEURS À 68500 BERGHOLTZ - FRANCE
PRODUCT OF FRANCE

## Loire Valley

Known as the "Garden of France," the Loire Valley offers a wide variety of wines produced from a plethora of grapes. The white grapes Chenin Blanc, Sauvignon Blanc, and Melon de Bourgogne lead the way. The individual appellations hug the Loire River as it dips and winds from the center of France until its destination in the Atlantic Ocean. The climate is generally cooler than other parts of the country and as a result many of the wines are lower in alcohol and lighter in body.

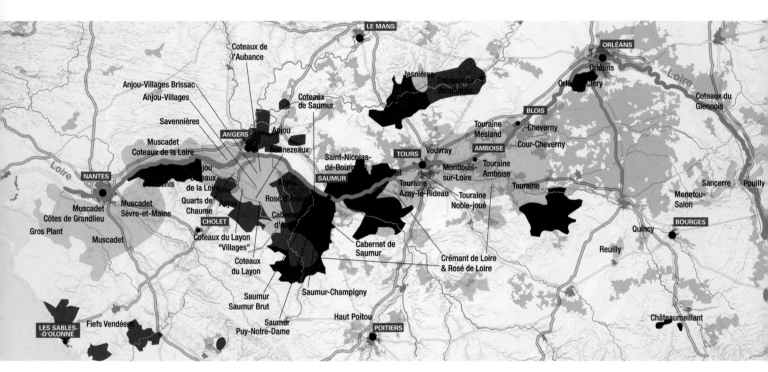

*The appellations of the Loire Valley.*

The longest river system in France, the Loire River spans more than 600 miles (965 km) from its origin in the Cévennes Mountains in southeast France. Classified as a "wild" river, its water level can vary by several yards within a few days, and the small islands within it move slowly each year. As it flows, the river carries with it numerous silt and mineral deposits. The warming effect it has in the autumn is helpful for ripening the grapes, which otherwise may fail to fully ripen given the northerly latitude of the vineyards.

From east to west, the Loire Valley winemaking appellations begin in the Central Vineyards, appropriately named due to their geographic location relative to the rest of France. The most important city is Orleans, best known as the city liberated from the English by Joan of Arc in 1429.

The major appellations for white wines are Pouilly-Fumé and Sancerre, both of which produce some of the best expressions of Sauvignon Blanc in the world. Locals feel that these wines are lighter and crisper compared to Sauvignon Blanc wines produced in New World countries.  Expect most of the wines to be light, fresh, and crisp. Very few are aged in barrels, as the influence of the oak tends to mask the unique aromas and tastes of Sauvignon Blanc, although some have earned cult-status, such as those by famed winemaker Didier Dagueneau.

Further downriver, Chenin Blanc is grown and used to produce wines in the appellation Vouvray. The wines vary from sparkling, dry *(sec)*, off-dry *(tendre)*, and sweet *(moelleux)*, depending upon the ripeness of the grapes each year and the philosophy of the winemaker. Regardless, it is widely agreed that there's no other place in the world where Chenin Blanc produces such elegant, structured, and complex wines. The key to these wines is acidity; even if the sugar is through the roof, the acidic profile of the wine helps maintain structure and gives the wines their zippiness.

As the Loire River approaches the Atlantic Ocean, Melon de Borgougne is grown to produce white wines labeled Muscadet. While not incredibly complex, the wines have found their niche in the crowded world of French wine. The wines are crisp and lean with briny and salty undertones. Some wines bear the term *sur lie*, indicating that the wines were in extended contact with the lees, the spent yeast cells from fermentation. This imbues a creamier complexion in the finished wine. More than 80 percent of all Muscadet wines are produced in the appellation Sèvre-et-Maine.

*Winemaking was first cited by the Gauls as far back as the first century. As the Loire River became a major trade route, wine was produced along the river and used as currency.*

*In the Loire valley, Sauvignon Blanc is also referred to as Blanc Fumé, a reference to the flinty and smoky notes in some of the wines. The term was later borrowed and commercialized by Robert Mondavi as his Fumé Blanc–labeled wines became the standard for California Sauvignon Blanc.*

## Rhône Valley

At its best, Viognier ranks high on the list of noble white grapes. Although less famous than Chardonnay and Riesling, the grape can produce equally stunning wines. Condrieu is a small appellation of about 330 acres (133 hectares) in the northern Rhône Valley where Viognier is the sole grape variety grown. Surrounded by other appellations that specialize in reds, Condrieu is a tiny region that seems like a white wine oasis in a sea of red. Dry, off-dry, or sweet, these wines are considered the end-all-and-be-all for Viognier. Usually quite expensive, the wines are intoxicating and floral with aromas of honey, ripe apricots, lush juicy pears, and pungent orange cream. Further south in the Rhône Valley, the white grapes Marsanne and Roussanne are grown in the appellations Hermitage and Crozes-Hermitage. The whites are pleasant and rich, with heavy mineral and chalky notes. Even further south, other white grapes such as Grenache Blanc, Bourboulenc, and Clairette are used to make white wines in Châteauneuf-du-Pape. They're also added in small portions to the reds in order to soften the harsh tannins of Syrah and Grenache.

The Rhône Valley is also known for its rosé wines, specifically in Tavel. Based on Grenache, the rosés are considered by many to be the world's best.

## Bordeaux

Bordeaux white wines are produced using Sémillon, Sauvignon Blanc, and Muscadelle. Dry whites from this area are never considered serious wines due to the popularity and significance of the reds from Bordeaux, but they're definitely worth a try. Since they're somewhat low on the totem pole, they're usually priced accordingly. Sémillon and Muscadelle are naturally higher in sugar levels and bring floral and honeysuckle notes to the wine and waxy textures. The crisp acidity of Sauvignon Blanc adds structure and body to the finished blend.

# Italy

Like its neighbor to the west, Italy produces nearly six billion bottles worth of wine each year. The conditions in Italy provide the seasonal changes necessary to grow vines throughout the entire country, yet much of the white wine production is in the north. The vineyards benefit from long, warm days of sunshine mixed with cold and brisk evenings from mountain drifts coming down from the Italian Alps. With hundreds of indigenous grapes, Italy remains one of the most challenging and exciting countries to navigate.

## Northwest

The Piedmont is home to Italy's most prized reds, but plenty of great white wines exist as well. Gavi is a wine named after the town of the same name, and by law must be produced using the grape Cortese. The wines are light- to medium-bodied with green hues. Most Gavi wines are crisp and lean; however, some producers are experimenting with oak aging. Other grapes include Erbaluce, Arneis, and Moscato, although Moscato is usually used for making *frizzante* and dessert wines.

*Harvesting Grenache Blanc grapes and loading them into the press in the Rhône Valley.*

*The famous gravel and pebbly soil of Bordeaux.*

The Valle d'Aosta is one of Italy's smallest regions. The elevation is so high that grapevines struggle to survive and those that do tend to produce less fruit. Petite Arvine, Pinot Grigio, and Prie Blanc lead the way for white grapes. Most of the wines are low alcohol and light and pale in color, a result of less-ripe grapes due to the cooler climate. What they lack in color and alcohol, they make up for in quality. Most of the producers who painstakingly pick the grapes from the steeply terraced vineyards do so with the utmost integrity, and the wines are as "boutique" as they come.

## Northeast

The most important appellations for Italian white wine production are all located in Friuli, Trentino-Alto Adige, and the Veneto. All three have perfect climates for white grape varieties and the soil composition is a mix of gravel, chalk, and limestone. These elements in the soil are expressed in the finished wines by aromas and flavors of flint, lime, and smoke. Add a little oak aging to the equation, and you've got the perfect recipe for age-worthy whites.

*Vineyards overlooking the Fontanafredda estate in the Piedmont.*

Friuli is the most northeastern region in Italy. Commonly grown grapes are Chardonnay, Sauvignon, and Pinot Bianco (Pinot Blanc). There is also a bevy of indigenous grapes such as Friulano, Ribolla Gialla, Malvasia, and Picolit. The ubiquitous Pinot Grigio, whether or not it is indigenous to Italy, has become synonymous with crisp and young Italian white wines. Needless to say, there's a lot to try from this region. Many producers' vineyards are positioned so that the warm winds blowing off the Adriatic Sea add warmth to the Alpine area, while the mountain air from the northwest keeps things cool at night. The rules for many of the appellations within Friuli are lax as to which grapes can be used, so it is common to find producers making a full range of wines from many different grapes. Furthermore, many of them also make blended wines, in some cases using many—or all—of the grapes they grow. Don't be surprised to find wines produced from four, five, or even more different types of grapes.

Trentino-Alto Adige is a very unique region within Italy. The soil is primarily volcanic bedrock with mineral deposits, known as quartz porphyry, located beneath a sandy and chalky topsoil. The sand is porous and thus provides the bedrock with sufficient water reserves for vines to sustain a drought season. The soil also retains heat from the daily sunshine and aids the vines during the cool nights in the area. Due to these conditions, many wines have a mineral profile that are bracing with acidity in their youth, and can properly age for decades longer than their counterparts from other areas of Italy. The common grapes are Sauvignon, Chardonnay, Traminer, Pinot Bianco, Moscato Gialla, Nosiola, Müller-Thurgau, and Sylvaner.

Of all twenty regions in Italy, the Veneto is one of the most productive, churning out tens of millions of bottles of wine every year, spread between sparkling (Prosecco), white (Soave), and red (Valpolicella). Soave is one of Italy's most historic white wine appellations. The dominant white grape variety used to make Soave is Garganega. The wines are quaffy, floral, and simple. They're excellent when paired with some of the local cheeses and cured meats. Thanks in part to the early popularity of Soave following World War II, Italian wines have been a major component of the international wine market.

*Snowcapped mountains overlooking the vineyards of Valter Scarbolo in Friuli.*

*Recommended Gavi producers:*

- *Pio Cesare*
- *Fontanafredda*
- *Martinetti*
- *La Battistina*
- *La Ghibellina*

---

*Winemakers are also farmers and blending grapes to make wine is an efficient way to use all the grapes each year. Before single variety wines became popular, blending was the order of the day. Blended wines are referred to as "field blends."*

---

*Pinot Grigio is classified as a white grape variety, but the skins of the grape are actually grayish and copper-toned. Traditionally, grapes were crushed and macerated with the skins throughout the fermentation process. This resulted in copper-toned, orange wines. Some producers in the northeast are now producing both styles of Pinot Grigio – one that sees no skin contact and is light and fresh, and one that has extended skin contact. The latter are called "ramato," translating to "copper" in Italian, a reference to the color of the wine. The wines are still refreshing and have the same profile of regular Pinot Grigio, although the skin contact results in a richer and fleshier mouthfeel.*

## Central Italy

Tuscany's most important white wine is Vernaccia di San Gimignano. Vernaccia, the grape, grows in and around the picturesque, hilltop town of San Gimignano. The wines are light and dry with peachy notes and herbal aromas. Closer to the coastline, Vermentino is the grape of choice. It grows better in the lower flat lands and sandier soils. The wines are medium to full and are comparable to the flavors and aromas of Riesling: petrol, orange peel, and bright acidity.

Verdicchio, an indigenous grape of Central Italy, is native to Le Marche, where it produces excellent wines with peach and pear fruit flavors. The wine serves as a perfect compliment to a classic Marchegiano fish "brodetto," or fish broth. Wines from Jesi, on the coast, are a bit more fleshy and lush, while wines from further inland in Matelica are racier and lighter.

Winemaking in Abruzzo is pretty simple. Most reds are made using Montepulciano and most whites are made using Trebbiano. Overall the wines are easy-going and ready to drink upon purchase. Two producers, however, have managed to achieve what no one else has been able to do with Trebbiano. Emidio Pepe and Edoardo Valentini earned global recognition for their wines and both men dominated the Abruzzese wine world for much of the latter half of the century. While most Trebbiano wines are light and simple, their white wines (and red wines for that matter) are complex, romantic, and age-worthy. They are meticulous in the vineyard, revolutionary in the winery, and consequently are immortalized in the world of wine.

Legendary winemaker Emidio Pepe harvesting Trebbiano grapes.

**Abboccato:** *slightly sweet*
**Amabile:** *semi-sweet*
**Appassimento:** *a method of drying grapes*
**Dolce:** *sweet*
**Frizzante:** *lightly sparkling*
**Passito:** *wine made with dried grapes, usually sweet*
**Secco:** *dry*
**Vendemmia Tardiva:** *late harvest*
**Vino liquoroso:** *fortified wine*
**Vin Santo:** *a sweet wine common in Tuscany*

Snow-covered vineyards in Abruzzo.

*Most Italian wines are labeled with the name of the grape and the city or town where it is produced. For example, "Morellino di Scansano" refers to the Morellino grape, which is produced in the town of Scansano.*

## Southern Italy and the Islands

Campania has not one, not two, but three indigenous grapes to try: Greco, Fiano, and Falanghina. Greco, or "little Greek one," is credited as being one of the genetic parents to many of the grapes used throughout Italy. It thrives around the town of Tufo and produces wines that are rich and viscous with flavors of pear and pine. Tufaceous volcanic soil, for which the town is named, provides calcium to the vines, yielding firm, flavorful wines. A layer of sand and clay beneath the tufa soil provides oxygen and drainage.

Fiano grows better further inland in the hills of Avellino, producing elegant wines with extreme aromatics of pineapple and long creamy finishes of nuts and earth. When aged in oak, wines can take on hints of spice and hazelnuts and can age gracefully for three to six years, gaining in depth and complexity.

*Vineyards in Noto in southeastern Sicily.*

Falanghina's name derives from Latin and means "stake" or "pole," referring to early trellising methods. It has piney fragrances matched by juicy grapefruit flavors. All three are great wines to try with some local *mozzarella di bufula*.

The sun-kissed islands of Sicily and Sardinia are home to many different types of grapes. Grillo, Inzolia, and Cataratto are grown throughout Sicily, but mostly in the west, where they produce light and fruity wines. Carricante is gaining in popularity; it is grown mostly in the east of Sicily, on the slopes of the highest active volcano in Europe, Mount Etna. The wines display a mix of ripe fruit with charred and ashy undertones, a direct result of the volcanic and ash soil. Sardinia is most known for the fresh and briny whites produced from the grapes Vermentino and Nuragus.

Producers on both islands must combat the scirocco, the fierce warming winds that blow off the coast of Africa. The sweltering heat and the velocity of the wind can cause irreparable damage to the vineyards, so some producers keep their vines trained low to the ground and use the leaves to shelter the grapes.

*Vineyards on the slopes of Mt. Etna in Sicily.*

# Spain

Spain, the third largest producer of wine, has a culture rooted in the enjoyment of food and wine. The climate and soil vary from region to region, with each specializing in different grapes. As a result, Spain offers a wide variety of wine styles ranging from sparkling, white, red, and fortified.

Other than Sherry, Spain's most important white wines come from the north. Galicia is a lush area bordering Portugal in the northwest of Spain. The land is a maze of rolling hills and forests divided by estuaries and rivers. The principal white wine grape is Albariño. It produces wines that are refreshing and sharp, with flavors of peaches, pears, and citrus. Those who like invigorating, acidic whites should embrace these teeth-chattering wines.

Within Galicia are five smaller appellations: Rías Baixas, Ribeiro, Valdeorras, Ribeira Sacra, and Monterrei. Of these five, Rías Baixas is the most popular, and wines from this appellation are easiest to find.

Located east of Galicia and in the center of the country is Rioja, Spain's most famous wine appellation. In 1991 it became the first winemaking zone to receive the country's highest denomination—Denominación de Origen Calificada (DOCa). Although more famous for its red wines, Rioja produces very popular and excellently made whites. The dominant grape for white wines is Viura, also known as Macabéo. Other grapes used for blending with Viura include: Garnacha Blanca, Malvasía Riojano, Maturana Blanca, Chardonnay, Sauvignon Blanc, and Verdejo.

*Spain's regulations for wine production are standardized throughout the country. Some of the more prestigious appellations, such as Rioja and Ribera del Duero, take it one step further and have their own, more detailed, regulations. On the whole, many of Spain's producers adhere to the wine categories listed in the table below.*

| Age Category | White Wine/Rosado Wine | Red Wine |
|---|---|---|
| *Vino Joven* | *Less aging required than Crianza* | *Less aging required than Crianza* |
| *Crianza* | *18 months (minimum 6 months in wood)* | *2 years (minimum 6 months in wood)* |
| *Reserva* | *2 years (minimum 6 months in wood)* | *3 years (minimum 6 months in wood)* |
| *Gran Reserva* | *5 years (minimum 18 months in wood)* | *4 years (minimum 6 months in wood)* |

Further south in Castilla y León, white wines from Rueda are based on the Verdejo grape. While historically a major part of Spanish wine, the grape fell out of favor with winemakers for some time due to a high propensity to oxidize—meaning the wines turned from crisp and refreshing to nutty and caramelized in a brief amount of time. Since the 1970s, however, producers have refocused their attention on Verdejo. Wineries have invested in modern technology and are more diligent in the vineyard. Around the same time, Sauvignon Blanc was introduced to the area. Now there is a full range of wines, some produced entirely from either one grape or the other and some produced by blending both grapes together.

*Spain has more land under vine than any other country, about three million acres (1,214,574 hectares).*

---

*Some recommended Rueda producers are:*

- *Marqués de Riscal*
- *Viños Sanz*
- *Alvarez y Díez*
- *Bodegas Antaño*

*German Rieslings have a reputation for being sweet. While there are many levels of sweetness, most German Rieslings are actually dry or off-dry with just a hint of sweetness. Many may taste "sweet" and "fruity," yet they are classified as dry wines. Only a small percentage of wine is made into dessert wines.*

---

*The term "residual sugar" does not always imply the wine will taste sweet and sugary. When properly made, the acidity in the wine outweighs the sugar component, and the wine tastes and feels dry. This is German winemaking at its best, with wines that are rich, full, and balanced.*

---

*A German wine zone is called an "anbaugebiete." Each* anbaugebiete *is further divided into* bereiches *(districts),* grosslagens *(general sites), and* einzellagens *(individual sites or vineyards).*

---

*The soil in Germany is crucial for proper grape development. The mix of blue slate and stone reflects the sunlight onto the vines during the day, and it also retains solar energy, which keeps the soil temperature warm throughout the evening and nights.*

---

*Look for these terms next time you're browsing the German wine aisle.*
**Trocken:** *dry*
**Halbtrocken:** *off-dry, half-dry, or medium-dry*

*Steeply terraced vineyards in Mosel, Germany.*

# Germany

Of all countries, Germany has the most unique laws regarding wine. In addition to geographic boundaries, there are classifications for ripeness and sugar levels in the grapes at the time of harvest. In theory this is a good idea, since the climate is cold and at the northern end of the spectrum for vine growth. Logic suggests that the riper the grape, the higher quality the wine will be. This is true in most cases, but the difficulty in interpreting the rule has made Germany a difficult country to understand for many wine beginners.

The following classifications for German wines are based on fruit ripeness at harvest from lowest sugar levels to highest sugar levels. While the highest level wines aren't necessarily the best, the winemakers have put more effort and resources into these grapes, and therefore they have the potential to make more complex and quality wines.

- Tafelwein (comprises less than 5 percent of overall production)
- Landwein
- Qualitätswein bestimmter Anbaugebiete (QbA)
- Qualitätswein mit Pradikat (QmP)

Within the highest category, QmP, are the following divisions:

- Kabinett: First QmP level; lowest alcoholic strength. Dry.
- Spatlese: Grapes are generally harvested two weeks later. Dry.
- Auslese: Selected harvest of individual bunches. Slightly sweet to sweet.
- Beerenauslese: Grapes affected by *botrytis* with high concentrations of sugar. Sweet.
- Trockenbeerenauslese (called TBA for short): Shriveled grapes from *botrytis cinerea*. Sweet.
- Eiswein: Grapes harvested and crushed while frozen. High extract and acidity.

There are thirteen major wine regions in Germany, many of them in the southwest part of the country. The best vineyards are in close proximity to the Rhine—Mosel, Neckar, Nabe, Saar, Ruwer, and Main Rivers. Most grapes are picked by hand, and many wineries are small, family-run properties.

Riesling, the most important white grape variety in Germany, grows in a variety of soils and climates, but the best expressions of the grape come from Mosel. Their elegance is unmatched, offering up aromas of petrol, orange citrus, and fresh herbs. They're some of the best transparent, complex, and age-worthy whites produced anywhere in the world. Other regions that specialize in Riesling are Rheingau, Pfalz, and Rheinhessen.

Other white grapes include: Kerner, Silvaner, Grauburgunder (Pinot Gris), Weissburgunder (Pinot Blanc), and Müller-Thurgau, which until 1996 was the most widely planted white grape variety. The honor now belongs to Riesling.

# Austria

Austria's main wine-growing regions are in the eastern half of the country where conditions are some of the driest in all of Europe. The vineyards zigzag through the valleys and hills, rubbing up against the borders of the Czech Republic, Slovakia, Hungary, and Slovenia. Austria is renowned for white wines from Riesling, Chardonnay, Müller-Thurgau, Sauvignon Blanc, Weissburgunder (Pinot Blanc), and Sylvaner. High elevation vineyards and cool climates produce sharp, fresh, light-bodied wines.

If you're looking for the absolute best to serve with your Austrian wiener schnitzel, go with a bottle made from the country's most important white grape, Grüner Veltliner. The grape is grown in all the major wine zones of Austria and accounts for more than 35 percent of all the wine produced annually. There are many different styles, ranging from light and dry to plump and off-dry. At its best, Grüner displays aromas of menthol, green pears, herbs, and graphite. Most of the wines are unoaked, and the ultra-crisp acidity makes them great pairings for all types of cuisines. The wines possess the freshness and zippiness of Pinot Grigio with the fruit and waxy aromas of Riesling.

*Hillside vineyards in the Wachau, Austria.*

Austria's wine regions from north to south are Lower Austria (Niederösterreich), Vienna (Wien), Burgenland, and Styria (Steiermark). Lower Austria is the country's largest area and over half the country's output is made here. Look for wines from some of the major appellations within Lower Austria such as Wachau, Kremsal, and Kamptal. The vineyards on the southern side of Austria in Styria are mostly planted to Sauvignon Blanc.

# Other European White Wines

Of all the wine from the **Czech Republic**, 80 percent is white, produced mostly from Müller-Thurgau, Riesling, Pinot Blanc, Sauvignon Blanc, and a native grape, Irsay Oliver. For the most part, the wines are light, aromatic, and fresh.

More than 3,000 acres (1,214 hectares) of vineyards grow in **England**, nearly double the amount in 2004. Most of the wine produced is either white or sparkling. The vineyards are at the northern limit for consistent grape production, and there will certainly be years with limited yields, but the English are more than eager to try their hand at viticulture. The country has been a net importer of wine for most of recorded history. It is about time the country reaps the benefits of its own vines. Müller-Thurgau is the most widely planted grape variety.

Other grapes grown include Seyval Blanc, Auxerrois, and Chasselas.

Most of the vineyards in **Greece** are in Macedonia and Peloponnese, although many of the islands are also dotted with some form of grapevines. Reds and whites are produced, but it is the flinty, steely, and saline whites from indigenous grapes—Assyrtiko, Robola, and Liatiko—that make Greece a unique stop for wine.

**Hungary**'s best wine region is centered on Lake Balaton in the west of the country. Indigenous white grapes Szürkeberát, Kéknyelü, and Furmint make pleasant wines, while the white grape Tokaji is mostly used to produce dessert wines.

**Portugal**'s main white appellation is Vinho Verde. The major grape varieties are Loureiro, Trajadura, Arinto, and Alvarinho. The wines are light, crisp, and bright. The Portuguese enjoy whites from this area, while aging their most important wine product, port, a fortified wine.

**Slovakia**'s wine trade revolves around simple and easy-going whites from Pinot Blanc, Müller-Thurgau, Silvaner, Traminer, and Sauvignon Blanc grapes. Wine enthusiasts are hopeful that the country can rise to prominence on the back of Tokaji, the same grape that Hungary grows to produce its trademark dessert wine.

**Slovenia**'s climate is similar to Northern Italy's and although only half of the wine is white, it is the better half of wine production. Grapes like Laski Rizling, Sauvignon Blanc, Ribolla Gialla, and Pinot Blanc are worth seeking out.

**Switzerland** exports only 10 percent of the wine it produces, and most of it is white, produced from the grape Chasselas. The warm winds blowing off Lake Geneva help keep the vineyards from freezing in the winter season. Wines are light in body and intended for immediate consumption. The best wines come from the western side of the country in the French-speaking cantons (wine zones) Valais, Vaud, Geneva, and Neuchâtel.

*Compared to German wines, Austrian whites have richer and fuller complexions because the weather is a bit warmer year round and the grapes can ripen more fully.*

*More than 80 percent of the wine produced in Austria is white.*

*When purchasing wines from Wachau in Lower Austria, here are the terms to know. The range is determined by the level of sugars in the grapes when picked from the vine*

- *Steinfeder – light and racy; maximum alcohol level of 11.5 percent*
- *Federspiel – elegant with firm body; alcohol between 11.5 percent and 12.5 percent*
- *Smaragd – very ripe and powerful; minimum alcohol level of 12.5 percent*

*In 2002, the Austria government introduced the DAC system, its own version of an appellation hierarchy similar to France, Italy, and the rest of Europe. DAC stands for Districtus Austriae Controllatus. Currently, there are eight approved DACs: Kamptal, Kremstal, Traisental, Weinviertel, Leithaberg, Mittelburgenland, Eisenberg, and Neusiedlersee.*

# A History of Wine Production in the United States

While not as colorful as Europe's winemaking past, the United States has a long and storied history of producing wine. Missionaries throughout California, Arizona, and New Mexico planted grapevines and made wine as early as the 1600s. Equally important were the contributions of settlers in the eastern United States, such as John James Dufour. Based in Ohio, Dufour started a cultural shift towards serious wine production in 1820 using Cape, a hybrid grape. While he failed to successfully grow *vinifera* grapes such as Cabernet Sauvignon and Merlot, his attempts didn't go unnoticed, and he is considered one of the founding fathers of American wine. He chronicled his experiences in *The American Vinedresser's Guide*, published in Cincinnati in 1826. Only 500 copies were printed.

*Thomas Jefferson, one of the country's most ardent believers in wine, tried in vain to produce world-class wines in Monticello, Virginia.*

Other immigrant settlers followed Dufour's lead, trying to incorporate grape growing and wine production that was such a huge part of their native European and South American cultures. When *phylloxera* devastated the vineyards in Europe, American grape growers prospered by supplying millions of rootstocks to European producers who were replanting their vineyards. Many of these American farmers were located in Ohio and Missouri, such as George Hussman, a leading activist in Missouri. Hussman advocated for wine production and the formation of horticulture boards. He went on to write books about wine and his experience growing vines in Missouri and California, where he founded the Oak Glen Winery. Thanks to his contributions, Missouri became a leading producer of wine in the latter half of the nineteenth century.

As European immigrants continued to settle in California, more wineries opened, some of which remain relevant to this day.

Paul Masson: Founded 1852 by Paul Masson of France

Beringer: Founded 1875 by Jacob and Frederick Beringer of Germany

Simi: Founded 1876 by Giuseppe and Pietro Simi of Italy

Inglenook: Founded 1879 by Gustave Niebaum of Finland

Throughout the country, wine production was taking off, and just when things looked bright, the 18th Amendment was enacted. The 1920 ruling prohibited alcoholic beverages from being produced and served. Thankfully, provisions in the Volstead Act permitted production within the household and intended solely for consumption within the household. Sacramental wine was permitted as well. Some wineries stayed afloat by selling concentrated grape juice to these ends.

It wasn't until fourteen years later that Prohibition was repealed. The wineries that survived were well positioned to make wine on a large scale and were the first to sell wine to an eager and insatiable public. Enter Ernest and Julio Gallo.

The Gallo family traces its roots to the Piedmont region in northern Italy, considered the best place for Italian wines. Ernest and Julio Gallo were quick to begin producing and selling wine following Prohibition's repeal in late 1933. They invested in more land for vines and equipment, such as industrial bottling machines. In 1942, they hired enologist Charles Crawford, the first of his kind, to oversee all wine production processes and improve quality.

The company grew rapidly and began researching different grape varieties and exploring alternative winemaking methods. In order to meet the growing demand, the brothers built glass and aluminum factories to produce their own glass bottles and screw caps. While blended wines from various grapes and vintages were a driving factor in their early success, they helped lead the charge for vintage-labeled, single-variety wines.

## The Judgment of Paris

The American wine market struggled during the Great Depression and through both World Wars, vexed by difficult economies and inequalities of supply and demand. The 1960s brought better days, and with them, better wines. The official debut party for the United States occurred at a wine competition in Paris in 1976. Coined "The Judgment of Paris," American red and white wines were tasted alongside French wines. A panel of esteemed French judges voted Stag's Leap Winery's Cabernet Sauvignon 1973 and Château Montelena's Chardonnay 1973 the best wines in their red and white categories, respectively. The judges tasted all the wines "blind," meaning they had no idea which wine they were evaluating, and ranked the wines from their favorite to their least favorite. Other wines in the tasting were produced by some of France's most influential estates, and the results of the tasting resonated around the world. After the competition, when quality wine was the topic of conversation, American wines were more than an afterthought—they were a major part of the discussion.

*Thompson Seedless was the most planted grape in California during Prohibition. Many of the home-brew kits sold throughout Prohibition were based on concentrate from this grape.*

*The E. and J. Gallo Wine Company is now the second largest wine company in the world, behind Treasury Wine Estates Limited of Australia. The company spans sixty different brands, employs more than 5,000 people, incorporates three generations of sixteen family members, and sells wine in more than ninety countries.*

## Other characters in the history of American wine are:

### Agoston Harazthy (1812–1869)

A Hungarian immigrant who founded the Buena Vista Winery in Sonoma in 1856, Harazthy was commissioned by the governor of California to travel through Europe and return with cuttings from quality vineyards. Although he left Europe en route to the US with 100,000 vines, only a fraction survived the trip home. Despite the setback, he was a luminary in California during his lifetime and helped fuel the fire for a transition to *vitis vinifera* grapes.

### Konstantin Frank (1899–1985)

Ukrainian-born Konstantin Frank helped create the wine industry in the eastern United States. Ahead of his time regarding viticulture, he was one of the first to design a system of covering grapevines during the colder months to prevent frost, a method that is still practiced today in many areas around the world. He ardently believed the future of American wines was rooted in *vinifera* grapes, rather than native *labrusca* varieties. Thanks to him, grapes like Riesling, Cabernet France, and Merlot are some of the more popular grape varieties grown throughout the eastern United States.

### Frank Schoonmaker (1905–1976)

A Princeton dropout who traveled throughout Europe during the Great Depression, Schoonmaker formed his own importing and distribution company that specialized in French and other European wines. He also advocated that California winemakers realize their potential by promoting California growing areas and varietal-labeled wines such as "Napa Valley Cabernet Sauvignon." Until this point, California was known mostly for bulk wines. He became a pivotal character in wine distribution and insisted that his domestic suppliers follow his suggestions for labeling their wines.

### Maynard Amerine (1911–1998)

An academic at the University of California at Davis, Amerine was one of the most important figures in grape growing and viticulture. With his colleague Albert Winkle, Amerine developed a heat summation index of California that helped identify the best areas to grow certain grapes, based on the heat and sunlight that certain areas historically received. The heat summation index has become the standard for researching new vineyard sites throughout the world. Amerine went on to write sixteen books and hundreds of articles covering all things wine.

### Robert Mondavi (1913–2008)

Originally from Minnesota, Mondavi helped elevate the status of American wines from mediocrity to center-stage. As a junior at Stanford University, he enrolled in chemistry and science classes, aiming to fulfill his father's prophecy of becoming a successful wine producer and merchant. During

Prohibition, his father purchased the Sunny Hill Winery in St. Helena, California, and renamed it Sunny St. Helena Winery. Robert set to work immediately and learned the trade. Although the winery specialized in bulk wine, Robert was eager to try his hand at producing more premium juice.

He admired the wines of the big four: Inglenook, Beaulieu Vineyards, Beringer Brothers, and Larkmead. Aiming to emulate their success, he purchased the Charles Krug Winery in 1943 for $75,000. After he hired André Tchelistcheff, a Russian-born grape and wine expert, the two men helped create and shape the model of success for all those who followed. They experimented with temperate-controlled fermentation tanks, sterile bottling, vacuum cleaning, extended skin contact, French barrique barrels, and a slew of other ideas. Mondavi designed an official "tasting room" and recreational area in 1950.

The success of the winery and the quality of the wines were immense. In 1965, he parted ways with his brother and the rest of the Mondavi family and began his own venture, the Robert Mondavi Winery. He would go on to work with many of the luminaries of the United States wine world, such as Warren Winiarski, Mike Grgich, and Zelma Lay, among others.

Thanks to his contributions, the United States changed its preference from sweet and fortified wines to high-quality, world-renowned wines. In 1966, California's 231 wineries produced 86 million gallons (325 million liters) of fortified wine and 55 million gallons (208 million liters) of dry table wine. In 1976, California's 345 wineries produced 13 million gallons (49 million liters) of fortified wine and an amazing 300 million gallons (1,135 million liters) of dry table wines.

*California wine pioneers from left to right: Robert Mondavi, Charles Forni, Madame Fernande de Latour, John Daniel Jr., and Al Huntinger.*

# New World White Wines

## United States

The United States is divided into appellations called American Viticultural Areas (AVAs). Within each zone, producers must follow certain rules and restrictions. For the most part, these rules are quite lax compared to many European appellation regulations.

### *California*

One of the nation's largest states, California has many different climates within its borders. Some are as cool as northern France and Germany, where Chardonnay, Riesling, and Pinot Noir are grown. Some are as hot as southern Europe, where conditions favor grapes such as Cabernet Sauvignon, Sangiovese, Merlot, Grenache, and Zinfandel. As a result, there are countless types of wine from California produced from a wide assortment of grapes. Don't let this bog you down. As your preferences develop, you'll gravitate towards the areas that are known for wines you prefer and stay away from those that produce wines you dislike.

There are five major wine-producing areas of California. Within each zone are numerous AVAs and sub-districts. From north to south the major areas are:

**North Coast:** Large enclave of hills and valleys north of San Francisco. Includes Napa, Sonoma, Mendocino, and Lake Counties.

**Primary grapes:** Cabernet Sauvignon, Merlot, Zinfandel, Syrah, Chardonnay, Sauvignon Blanc, Riesling

**Sierra Foothills:** East of Sacramento. Includes Yuba, Nevada, Placer, El Dorado, Amador, Calaveras, Tuolumne, and Mariposa Counties.

**Primary grapes:** Cabernet Sauvignon, Zinfandel, Chardonnay, Sauvignon Blanc, Riesling, Muscat

**Central Valley:** Huge inland growing area. The area encompasses more than 55 percent of all the vineyards in the state and accounts for more than 75 percent of all the wine produced. Known for jug wines and lesser quality table wines, the area might improve the quality in the years to come. However, critics feel that the geography and climate are best suited for lower quality wines. The variety of grapes grown here is variable.

**Central Coast:** Vast stretch of land from San Francisco in the north to Santa Barbara in the south. Major appellations are based south of San Francisco, south of Monterey, and north of Santa Barbara.

**Primary grapes:**  Zinfandel, Chardonnay, Sauvignon Blanc, Cabernet Sauvignon, Merlot

**South Coast:** The area is more historically significant than the wine that comes out of the region. Once known for its fortified wines in the mid-nineteenth century, today's wines from this area are interesting but simple.

**Primary grapes:** Chardonnay, Sauvignon Blanc, Chenin Blanc, Cabernet Sauvignon, Riesling, Merlot, Zinfandel

*California produces about 90 percent of all wine in the United States. If California were its own nation, it would rank fourth in total wine production.*

*Wire-trellised vineyards of Riesling grapes.*

## Navigating the California Wine Label

*Below are some terms that producers in California's 107 AVAs must incorporate onto their wine labels.*

- **Varietal-labeled** *wine must be made from at least 75 percent of the named grape. Until 1983, the minimum was only 51 percent.*

- **AVA-designated** *wines must be produced using at least 85 percent of grapes from the district indicated. For example, "Paso Robles Zinfandel" must be made from at least 85 percent Zinfandel grapes grown within the Paso Robles AVA.*

- **Vineyard-designated** *wines must be produced from at least 95 percent of grapes from the specified vineyard.*

- **Estate-bottled** *wines must be made by wineries that own or control all the vineyards where the grapes are grown. The winery crushes, ferments, and produces the wine in one continuous process. This is an important distinction because the main gap in a quality wine versus a mediocre wine arises when wineries purchase grapes or juice from another source. The guarantee of estate-bottled wines means that the winery has had total control of each and every grape that went into the production of the bottle.*

- **Vintage-labeled** *wines must be produced from at least 95 percent of grapes from the indicated vintage.*

- **Additional label requirements** *include the brand name, the address and location where the wine was bottled, health warnings, and sulfite and alcohol content.*

## California's Major White Grapes

The main white grapes of California are Chardonnay and Sauvignon Blanc, followed by Riesling, Viognier, Chenin Blanc, and Pinot Blanc.

Chardonnay is the most widely planted grape variety with 95,000 acres (38,445 hectares) under vine, about one-fifth of all California's total vineyard space. For a long time, California Chardonnay was the epitome of rich, creamy, buttery, and oaky. Modeled after the white wines of Burgundy, France, this style of Chardonnay grew in popularity. Critics loved them and the consumers loved them even more. Throughout the 1990s and early 2000s, the favorable reviews poured in, and more California Chardonnay producers turned to producing this style of wine. Eventually there was a tipping point. In efforts to "out-oak" the competition, some wineries overdid it and churned out "oak bombs," wines that overpowered the grape's natural flavor and aromas.

In what seems like the blink of an eye, the world has turned its back on rich, oaky Chardonnay, and many wineries have responded by dialing down on the oak treatment. Instead of maturing their wines in small and new French oak barrels each year, they're opting for a combination of different-sized barrels, some new and some used, to produce wines that have the kiss of oak, yet still offer up fresh appley fruit flavors.

Riesling and Viognier can produce elegant and wonderfully structured wines, but when produced poorly they taste overly sweet and sticky, lacking the crucial acidity needed to keep the wine intact. In the words of Jay McInerney, "When fruit outweighs acidity, [wines] can be reminiscent of syrup at the bottom of canned fruit salad."

## North Coast

Napa Valley is known for its red wines, but also produces excellent whites. You can find Sauvignon Blanc and Chardonnay wines throughout the area. Some of the best white wines are from Carneros, in southern Napa County. The coolest area of Napa, it is where Chardonnay produces both dry and sparkling wines. To the west, the hub for whites in Sonoma County is in the Russian River Valley appellation, where cool breezes and fog roll in from the Pacific Ocean. Unlike Napa and Sonoma, Mendocino County is cooler in the north, and grapes like Riesling, Gewurztraminer, and Sauvignon Blanc consistently ripen slowly, especially in the Alexander Valley appellation. Lake County is the least known area of the North Coast, but pleasant Sauvignon Blanc and Chardonnay wines are produced here.

*There are more than 1,600 wineries in California, up from 231 in 1966.*

*Be wary of wines that say "California Wine" and bear no other type of appellation or geographic designation. California is vast, and the wine is probably a blend of different grapes sourced from a variety of places.*

## Central Coast

There are many historic estates in the Bay Area south of San Francisco. Wineries such as the Wente Estate in Alameda County, and Mount Eden, Ridge, and Bonny Doon in the Santa Cruz Mountains appellation have helped shape the landscape of American wine. The coastal influence and the rugged terrain are best suited for Chardonnay and Sauvignon Blanc.

The Monterey region between San Francisco and Santa Barbara is planted to a wide variety of grapes. Chardonnay and Pinot Bianco are good bets from within the Santa Lucia Highlands appellation. Chalone, the furthest appellation inland, is named after the famed Chalone Estate. Plantings date back to the 1940s and are planted in a mix of limestone and granite—ideal for Chardonnay, Pinot Blanc, and Chenin Blanc. The Chardonnay wines are highly sought after, as are the reds produced from Pinot Noir. Located within the Mount Harlan appellation, the Calera winery is credited with planting the first Viognier vines in the area.

The southernmost area of the Central Coast is thriving with new plantings and new and exciting wines. The appellations within San Luis Obispo County have garnered a lot of attention due to beloved wines based on Viogner and Chardonnay. Look for wines from the following appellations: Paso Robles, York Mountain, Edna Valley, and Arroyo Grande. South of these in Santa Barbara County, Chardonnay, Riesling, Chenin Blanc, Sauvignon Blanc, and Gewürtraminer are planted throughout the two main appellations, Santa Maria Valley and Santa Ynez Valley.

*Dundee Hills, Oregon.*

## Oregon

Of Oregon's sixteen AVAs, the Willamette Valley is the state's most prolific. Further south and closer to the border with California are the Umpqua, Rogue, and Applegate Valleys. Bordering Washington, the Columbia Valley and Walla Walla Valley appellations are shared with the neighboring state. While Chardonnay once prevailed, Pinot Gris (Pinot Grigio) has become the darling white grape of Oregon. It grows throughout the state, and the best wines have flavors of citrus fruits and crisp, refreshing acidity. Pinot Blanc, Sauvignon Blanc, Seyval Blanc, Riesling, Chardonnay, and Sémillon are also grown.

## Washington State

More than thirty grape varieties in Washington are made into wine. The main white varieties are Riesling, Chardonnay, Pinot Gris, Sauvignon Blanc, Gewürztraminer, Viognier, Sémillon, and Chenin Blanc. Riesling was once considered the white variety of Washington, but wines from other grapes have made bigger headlines lately, and producers are re-evaluating their land and which grapes to grow. Just more than half of all the wine produced in the state is white; the majority of the wines are light- to medium-bodied and generally consumed in their youth. A few producers specialize in barrel-fermented Sémillon that can age well for a few years.

Puget Sound, located on the eastern side of the Cascade Mountains, is remarkably wetter and cooler than all the other appellations within the state. Although few vineyards exist in Puget Sound, many of the state's wineries and tasting rooms are located there, benefiting from the tourism generated from Seattle, Tacoma, and other coastal cities. Columbia Crest, Seven Hills, Leonetti Cellar, Kiona, Cougar Crest, and Château Ste. Michelle wineries all produce a wide range of wines that are great introductions to the wines of Washington State. Château Ste. Michelle is Washington's oldest and largest winery, dating to 1934.

*Oregon is one the strictest states in the nation regarding labeling laws.*

- *If a grape variety is stated on the label, the wine must be made from at least 90 percent of the specific grape, except for Cabernet Sauvignon, which can have 75 percent.*
- *If a vintage is stated on the label, 95 percent of the wine must be produced from that vintage.*
- *If an AVA is stated on the label, 100 percent of the grapes must come from that appellation.*

---

*Many elite winemakers from abroad are focusing some of their time and efforts in Washington, working with Washington's wineries as consulting advisors. A few are listed below.*

- *Col Solare - Renzo Cotarella (Italy)*
- *Pedastal - Michel Rolland (France)*
- *Château Ste. Michelle - Ernst Loosen (Germany)*
- *Sequal - John Duval (Australia)*

*Some of New York's white grape varieties include:*

- *Vitis Vinifera: Riesling, Chardonnay, Pinot Blanc, and Gewürztraminer*
- *Vitis Labrusca: Elvira, Noah, Niagara, and Duchess*
- *Hybrids: Seyval Blanc, Vidal Blanc, Ravat Blanc, and Vignoles*

## New York

The hub for wines from the eastern United States, New York has summers hot enough to grow vines, but the winters can be devastatingly cold, so cold that the grapevines can perish. As a result, New York winemakers grow a variety of grapevines, spanning the *vinifera* varieties such as Riesling and Chardonnay, to indigenous American vines such as Concord, to hybrids such as Seyval Blanc.

Grapevines have been a part of the New York landscape for hundreds of years, but only recently has quality made its way to the market. Dr. Konstantin Frank was the first to prove that quality vinifera grapes could successfully be grown in the cool climate and produce elegant and structured wines to rival Europe's best. Before this, most wines were made from hybrids and *labrusca* grapes, which are commonly described as "foxy" or "grapey." While wines from these grapes can be interesting, most enthusiasts snub them.

Throughout the first half of the 1950s, Dr. Frank worked closely with legendary Champagne master Charles Fournier and helped put New York wines on the map. He eventually started his own winery, eponymously named Dr. Konstantin Frank. His success encouraged others to plant the superior *vinifera* varieties, and now the Finger Lake and Lake Erie appellations produce some of the best whites in the state. Most are produced from Riesling, Chardonnay, and Gewürztraminer grapes.

*Vineyards in the Finger Lakes, NY.*

## Other States

Every state in the nation has at least one winery; some grow their own grapes, while others simply buy either the juice or grapes and produce wine.

Here are some important wine-producing states and the white wines on which they focus.

| State | Grape |
| --- | --- |
| Connecticut | Seyval Blanc, Vidal Blanc Chardonnay, Riesling, Cayuga, Aurora |
| Indiana | Chardonnay, Seyval Blanc, Vidal Blanc, Vignoles, Aurora |
| Maryland | Seyval Blanc, Vidal Blanc, Chardonel, Riesling |
| Massachusetts | Seyval Blanc, Vidal Blanc, Cayuga, Aurora, Chardonnay, Riesling |
| Michigan | Niagara, Pinot Gris, Gewürztraminer, Riesling |
| New Hampshire | Seyval Blanc, Chardonnay, Riesling, LaCrosse, LaCrescent |
| New Jersey | Seyval Blanc, Vidal Blanc, Chardonnay, Riesling |
| New Mexico | Chardonnay, Riesling, Sauvignon Blanc, Pinot Grigio |
| Ohio | Niagara, Chardonnay, Riesling, Gewürztraminer, Seyval Blanc |
| Pennsylvania | Seyval Blanc, Cayuga, Vidal Blanc, Chardonnay, Pinot Grigio, Riesling |
| Rhode Island | Vidal Blanc, Seyval Blanc, Cayuga, Chardonnay, Riesling |
| Texas | Chardonnay, Chenin Blanc, Muscat, Riesling, Sauvignon Blanc, Sémillon, Gewürztraminer, Vidal Blanc |
| Virginia | Pinot Grigio, Sauvignon Blanc, Viognier, Riesling, Seyval Blanc, Vidal Blanc |

# Canada

Only a few areas of Canada are warm enough to grow grapes, most of which are in the south along the U.S. border. There are four main wine-producing areas: Ontario, British Columbia, Quebec, and Nova Scotia. The majority of Canada's wine comes from southern Ontario within four Designated Viticultural Areas (DVAs): Pelee Island, Lake Erie North Shore, Niagara Peninsula, and Prince Edward County. *Vinifera* varieties like Chardonnay, Riesling, Sauvignon Blanc, and Pinot Grigio grow well in the cooler climates of Canada. Hybrid grapes such as Seyval Blanc are also popular because they're more resilient to the challenging weather conditions. Vidal Blanc, another hybrid grape, is used to make Canada's famous syrupy ice wine.

*Canada consumes seven times more wine than it produces.*

*Vineyard growing in Mendoza Valley, Argentina.*

*Rising 6,000 feet (2 km) above sea level, vineyards in Salta are among the highest elevated vineyards in the world.*

# Argentina

Argentina's high elevation vineyards on the slopes of the Andes Mountains provide the ideal conditions for producing fresh, clean, mineral white wines. The cool temperatures help the grapes ripen slowly which concentrates flavors in the grapes.

The main white variety, Torrontés, is grown throughout the country where it produces wines with good acidity and structure; however, the bulk of the best wines are grown in Salta in the northern provinces of Argentina. The average elevation in Argentina for vineyards is about 2,700 feet (823 m) above sea level. The cool nights at such high elevations preserves the natural acids of the grapes, resulting in extremely pleasant and affordable whites. Pinot Grigio, Chardonnay, and Chenin Blanc are also grown throughout the country.

# Chile

White grapes grow especially well in the cooler areas of Chile, such as Casablanca. Prolific fog resulting from the cool mountain air colliding with warm sea winds helps protect the grapes from the scorching rays of the sun. Chardonnay and Sauvignon Vert (not exactly the Sauvignon Blanc we're used to, but similar in style) are most popular. Most Sauvignon wines lack the trademark grassy and peppery notes that are more common in France and New Zealand, but they're loaded with acidity, fresh green fruits, and saline finishes.

As one heads further south, the temperatures generally are lower and white grapes are popular choices in the Maipo, Rapel, and Maule Valleys. These are Chile's most important zones, and white grapes and black grapes are sporadically intertwined in the vineyards. In what was once red wine country, Chile now offers a drastically improved selection of whites, specifically from Chardonnay and Sauvignon. The zone furthest south for quality wines is Bío Bío, where Muscat is the most widely planted grape.

In 2011, the Chilean Ministry of Agriculture created three terms to help identify and promote its wines. "Costa" is used for wines produced from grapes that grow near the coastline, "Andes" can be applied to wines produced in close proximity to the mountains, and "Entre Cordilleras" is for those produced between the two.

# Brazil

Grapevines were first cultivated by Portuguese colonists in the sixteenth century, but withered when the Christian missionary buildings were destroyed and vacated. The current state of winemaking in Brazil dates to the late 1800s when Italian immigrants brought with them their love of the vine. There are now more than 1,100 wineries throughout the country's six wine regions, most of which are located in the south, far from the equator, bordering with Uruguay and Paraguay. The main white varieties are Chardonnay, Riesling, Sémillon, and Gewürztraminer.

*Organic vineyard in Chile's Casablanca Valley.*

# Australia

Captain Arthur Philip imported Australia's first grapevines from Brazil and South Africa in 1788. Shortly after, the first commercial wine was produced just south of Sydney in the early 19th century. Grapes like Pinot Gris, Verdelho, and Sémillon were preferred. The first exported wine to the United Kingdom was recorded in 1822, about 183 bottles' worth. Almost 200 years later, the United Kingdom is still buying wines from Australia. Recently, Australia overtook France as the leading supplier of wines to the United Kingdom. It is also the second leading exporter of wines to the United States, behind Italy.

The stereotype of Australian white wines is that all Chardonnays are dark gold in color and rich and creamy from long maturation in new oak barrels. While there may be many wines like this, Australia's leading wine experts feel that the pendulum is swinging back to making wines that speak less about the winemaking process and more about the provenance of the grapes, in the true sense of the word.

*Sunrise peaks over the hills in South Australia.*

The ease of navigating Australian wine labels has helped the country become an exporting machine. Contrary to Europe's archaic labeling system, Australia's is rather simple. Geographic Indicators (GIs) are geographic boundaries for wine production, but within these zones there is nothing that dictates which grapes can be grown nor are there rigorous restrictions on winemaking techniques. If a wine is labeled with a certain grape variety, the wine must be produced from at least 85 percent of that grape. If it is a blended wine, producers must list the blend in descending order. If a specific GI is listed on the label, at least 85 percent of the grapes much come from that location, and if a vintage is given, then at least 95 percent of the grapes must be of that vintage.

Many of Australia's wine regions produce both reds and whites, but the best of the whites come from the cooler, high-elevation vineyards throughout the coastal regions. The vineyards of western Australia are isolated in the southwestern tip of the continent, nearly 1,000 miles (1,600 km) away from the next closest appellation in South Australia. What the region lacks in volume it makes up for in quality. Many of the producers are smaller estates and focus on Chardonnay, Cabernet Sauvignon, and Merlot. Accounting for less than 5 percent of all the wine produced in Australia, there are plenty of fun and interesting wines to discover. Margaret River, the most popular winemaking appellation, is known for making wines of elegance and grace, rather than power and depth. Other appellations include Great Southern, Pemberton, Geographe, and Swan Valley.

South Australia is home to some of the country's most important wines. Most of the area is planted to Shiraz and Cabernet Sauvignon, and the big, brooding reds are Australia's specialty. Most of these vineyards are at lower elevations where the grapes soak up the hot sun. Other appellations like Adelaide Hills and Kangaroo Island are growing in vineyard acreage as growers look to these cooler climates for growing grapes like Sauvignon Blanc, Riesling, Chardonnay, and Sémillon. Sauvignon Blanc from South Australia is generally less aromatic than New Zealand Sauvignon Blanc, and show less aromas of kiwi and lanolin. Australian winemaker Michael Hill Smith describes them as "lean without being skinny."

Tasmania is a small island off the southeastern coast. Many of its vineyards are located on the east side of the island, as the western half is too wet and cool to grow vines. Since this area is at the southern extreme for cultivating vines, frost and hail are problematic, as are harsh sea winds that blow off the coastline. Screens are necessary in some places to protect the grapes from these damaging coastal sea winds. Cool climate grapes like Chardonnay, Riesling, and Pinot Noir are cultivated.

Efforts are also underway to produce high-quality and premium sparkling wines. There are more than 100 producers in Tasmania, although the total amount of wine produced on this island is less than that of some single wineries on the mainland. Given that commercial winemaking is relatively new to this area, many of Tasmania's best vineyards have yet to be planted.

*Although there are more than 3,000 producers in Australia, 80 percent of the wine is produced by five large companies with multiple holdings (Southcorp, BRL Hardy, Orlando Wyndham, Beringer Blass, and McGuigan Simeon).*

———

*Try these producers from western Australia:*

- *Moss Wood Wines*
- *Robert Oatley*
- *Xanadu*

———

*A $25 million National Wine Center was built in Adelaide in 2001. It hosts 170,000 visitors each year, offering tastings, education, and promotion of Australia's booming wine industry.*

*Innovation is abounding in New Zealand. There's still a lot of experimentation occurring in the vineyards regarding which grapes to grow and produce into wine. Producers are sticking with cool climate grapes such as Pinot Noir, Chardonnay, and Riesling, but new plantings of other grape varieties persists. A group of self-governing growers and wineries developed a code of practice called the New Zealand Integrated Winegrape Production (NZIWP). Members of this organization help promote the environmental importance and benefits of sustainable farming and cultivation, a positive sign that a long-term wine culture is in the works. Not all the initiatives are focused only on farming. In 2002, The New Zealand Winegrowers organization was established as a joint venture project between the New Zealand Grape Growers Council and The Wine Institute of New Zealand. Its aim is to provide a uniform platform for promoting the wines of New Zealand to create a strong and dynamic wine industry.*

---

*The first grape from Australia to achieve international success was Sauvignon Blanc, and many of the best wines come from the Marlborough appellation. Until then, France's Loire Valley had been the premier and pretty much the only appellation for upper-echelon Sauvignon Blanc. Wines from Marlborough are usually more full-bodied and richer, and exhibit tropical fruit flavors erring more on the side of kiwi, mango, and in some cases, jalapeño notes. The wines from France are a bit leaner, offer more acidity and firmness, and are drier with more flinty and mineral notes. Currently Sauvignon Blanc comprises more than half of all New Zealand's vineyards, totaling more than 45,000 acres (17,000 hectares).*

# New Zealand

New Zealand is a relative newcomer to the international wine market. Grapevines have been cultivated for hundreds of years ever since the Maoris, from the Polynesians islands, first inhabited the area. Only recently, though, have producers realized the potential of New Zealand's climate and soil. Beginning in the mid 1800s, when conventional grape growing first began, farmers relied on North America varieties. They were easier to cultivate, more resistant to disease, and produced higher yields. Over the next hundred years, grape growing flourished, but with mixed results. There was a heavy focus on quantity, and only a fraction of the grapes made their way into quality table wine. The rest was used for plump and inexpensive dessert wines, or "stickies," mostly made from the productive and reliable Müller-Thurgau grape.

As one of the world's newer formed land masses, New Zealand has young and rigid mountain ranges, lush valley floors, and mineral-rich soils. The soil provides vitality and youthful energy—a pivotal combination for a young grapevine as it aims to establish a solid root system in its infancy. The ocean has a profound effect on all areas of the country. From any location on North or South Island, it is at most 70 miles (112 km) to the nearest coastline. The Pacific Ocean and Tasman Sea generate clouds that produce precipitation, which is pivotal in some of the drier parts of the country.

## *North Island*

Auckland is the center for white wine production on the north island, specifically in the sub-regions of Henderson, Kumeu, and Huapai. With 50 inches (127 cm) of rain per year, the surplus of water can lead to diluted grapes, but wineries have learned to grow cover crops to reduce this surplus. The more popular grapes of choice are Chardonnay, Riesling, and Sauvignon Blanc. Gisborne is southeast of Auckland, and the better whites are produced from Chardonnay, Gewürztraminer, Viognier, and Pinot Gris.

The southernmost winemaking zone on North Island is Wairarapa, which spans about 21 miles (34 km). The region can be further divided into three smaller zones: Masterton, Gladstone, and Martinborough. A variety of grapes are grown, including Chardonnay, Pinot Noir, Riesling, and Gewürztraminer, but the main attraction is Sauvignon Blanc.

## South Island

Marlborough is the most famous appellation of New Zealand. The success stories of Marlborough wines have no doubt helped initiate growth and new vineyard plantings elsewhere throughout the country. The soil is loose and gravely, providing excellent water drainage for vines. The sunlight hours are long during the summer months, and the autumn season is cool and dry. This kind of climate helps the grapes develop sugars during the day and aids in the retention of natural acids.

Sauvignon Blanc from Marlborough is New Zealand's most prized wine, and has helped catapult the country from an aspiring neophyte to proven trendsetter. The wines are lush, juicy, and herbaceous, hitting on the flavor profile of those who prefer richer wines; but they express mineral and acidic notes, characteristics preferred by the traditional connoisseurs. Also look for wines made from Chardonnay, Gewürztraminer, Pinot Gris, and Riesling.

Nelson, the next closest winemaking zone, is just a stone's throw to the north from Marlborough. As the apple industry in Nelson has declined, vineyards have been replacing the orchards and more wineries are starting operations. What it lacks in scope, it makes up for in fortitude, and the results have been worldwide renown and acclaim for the aromatic white wines produced from Riesling, Gewürztraminer, Pinot Gris, and Sauvignon Blanc.

*Vineyards at Felton Road in Central Otago, New Zealand.*

# South Africa

Most of South Africa's vineyards are on the southern coast around Cape Town. Like many New World countries, South Africa actually has a long history of wine production, but many of the wines were low quality and failed to compete inside its own borders, let alone make a ripple outside its borders.

The most widely planted grape is Chenin Blanc, accounting for one fifth of all vineyards. Known locally as Steen, the wines are plump and fruity with lower levels of acidity, akin to the whites of the Loire Valley, where it is believed the best Chenin Blanc wines are made. The South African expressions of the grape are pleasant and are getting much better year after year as profits are reinvested into better vineyard mechanics and winemaking equipment. Many of the world's elite winemakers are coming to South Africa on a consultancy basis to offer assistance as well, aiding in the quality revolution. Other white varieties ("cultivars" as they're called in South Africa) have been growing in acreage and are moving in on Chenin Blanc's dominance. Producers are crafting simple, yet delicious wines from Chardonnay, Sauvignon Blanc, Colombard, Riesling, and Viognier.

South Africa is still undergoing major soul searching, but the climate, soil, and passion are all in place, and the future looks bright for South African wines. It continues to be one of the countries with a wide selection of reliable, food-friendly, and affordable wines. In the words of wine writer Oz Clarke, "justifiable self-confidence is taking the place of complacency."

Seven South African whites that won't break the bank:

1. Stellenbosch Vineyards – "Oracle" Sauvignon Blanc
2. De Trafford – Chenin Blanc
3. Warwick Estate – "Professor Black" Sauvignon Blanc
4. Joostenberg Wines – "Family Blend" Chenin Blanc/Viognier
5. Six Hats – Sauvignon Blanc
6. A.A Badenhorst – "Secateur" Chenin Blanc
7. Franschhoek Cellars – Chardonnay

---

South Africa's first wine was made on February 2, 1659. One of the country's most influential and historical Dutch settlers, Jan van Riebeeck, documented the first pressing of wine from the Cape variety in his journal.

---

In 2005, South Africa exported nearly thirty-two million cases of wine, up from about six million cases in 1994.

Vineyards in Montague, South Africa.

# Old World Red Wines

## France

### *Bordeaux*

Red wines from Bordeaux are the benchmark for all red wines in the world. Based on Cabernet Sauvignon and Merlot, they've been the most important wines for hundreds of years, ever since the Dutch built levees and docks and drained much of the land now called the Médoc. Prior to this, many wines were produced further up river in the Graves district. The region was a hotbed for wine due to its easy access by river to the rest of Europe. Between 1152 and 1453, Britain ruled Bordeaux. As British influence expanded to the corners of the world, so did the reach of Bordeaux wine.

The wine world is riddled with appellations, rules, and classifications, but none are more significant than the Bordeaux Classification of 1855. In anticipation of the World's Fair, Emperor Napoléon III asked that the wines of Bordeaux be ranked to aid visitors. Sixty châteaux from the Médoc and one from Graves were codified according

*Bordeaux wines are sometimes described as either "left bank" or "right bank," referring to the banks of the Gironde and Dordogne Rivers. Left bank wines are based on Cabernet Sauvingon, while right bank wines are based on Merlot and Cabernet Franc. Other grapes that can be used in small amounts are Petit Verdot, Malbec, and Carmenère.*

*Bordeaux is the world's most prestigious wine zone. More than 13,000 growers produce 850 million bottles each year.*

*The façade of Château Phélan-Ségur in St. Estèphe, Bordeaux.*

to the prices they commanded at the time. They were assigned to one of five classes, ranging from the most esteemed and expensive, First Growth, down to the least expensive, Fifth Growth. Since that time, these sixty-one producers have been held in the highest regard and have set the bar for other châteaux that followed. It is not to say that these are still the best wines to be found in Bordeaux to this day, but they're always a part of the discussion.

The appellations of the Left Bank in Bordeaux are planted mostly to Cabernet Sauvignon, where the vines thrive in gravel soils. Saint-Estèphe, Pauillac, Saint-Julien, Listrac, Moulis, and Marguax are the main appellations, and many of the best and famous red wines in the world are crafted here.

The appellations of the Right Bank are planted mostly to Merlot and Cabernet Franc. The soil is composed of limestone and clay, and these grapes grow better in this damper and cooler soil. The two most important appellations are St.-Émilion and Pomerol, where smaller producers have entered the market, generating a cult following for their ultra-ripe and collectable wines.

Red Bordeaux wines are usually made by blending wines from different grapes. The final blend changes every year depending upon the quality of each grape type. The grapes are picked and fermented separately and then blended after fermentation. Aging in small, new oak barrels is common, which give the wines strong tannin profiles and age-ability. Many different styles of young Bordeaux exist, but one can expect dark cassis fruits, oaky cherry flavors, and graphite aromas.

*The barrel room at Château Phélan-Ségur in St. Estèphe, Bordeaux.*

*It is said that Bordeaux is for intellectuals and men and women of patience and reason. The wines develop complexity and grace over time. Burgundy is for the lover, the lunatic, and the poet. It engages the emotions and senses more than the intellect.*

---

*Beaujolais Nouveau helped create demand for wines from this region, although it came at a price. "Nouveau" wine is fresh wine from the recent harvest, always released on the third Thursday in November. The fruitiness and ease of Gamay lends itself to this style of wine, but the popularity of the cheap and easy-going wine has tarnished the higher-end spectrum of Beaujolais reds.*

---

*For the best in Beaujolias, try wines from one of the ten crus from the northern half of the appellation.*

1. *St-Amour*
2. *Juliénas*
3. *Moulin-a-Vent*
4. *Chénas*
5. *Fleurie*
6. *Chiroubles*
7. *Morgon*
8. *Régnié*
9. *Brouilly*
10. *Côte de Brouilly*

## Burgundy

Pinot Noir is the main grape used in Burgundy, France to produce red wines. All other Pinot Noir wines look to Burgundy as the epitome of Pinot Noir expression. Young, fresh, and gentle in its youth, red Burgundy evolves into smoky, beefy, lavender, complex wines after aging. Some red wines from Burgundy are among the most expensive and sought-after wines in the world, commanding insane prices at auctions. Gamay is the second black grape of Burgundy, where it is grown in the south and used to make wines labeled "Beaujolais."

*Vineyards at Château du clos de Vougeot in Burgundy, France. Originally a wine farm built by the monks at the nearby Abbey of Cîteaux, the château was constructed in the 16th century.*

The grape grows throughout the northern appellations of Burgundy, specifically in the northern half of the Côte d'Or, called the Côte de Nuits. The villages are intertwined as the valley dips and winds from north to south. The main villages are Marsannay, Fixin, Gevrey-Chambertin, Morey-St-Denis, Chambolle-Musigny, Vougeot, Vosne-Romanée, and Nuits-St-Georges. Within these prestigious villages, there are even more elite vineyards. Almost all of the vineyards are owned by more than one grower. This style of split ownership allows a Burgundy connoisseur to taste several different wines from within the same vineyard, each produced by a different winery that picks the grapes at different times and crafts the wine according to different beliefs.

Similar to white wines of Burgundy, certain vineyards are held in higher regard than others. The Grand Cru vineyards are most significant. These 24 vineyards are viewed as holy lands with the best soil content and exposure to the sun, and consequently they command the highest prices. The Premier Cru vineyards are considered less prestigious on paper, although the wines from these vineyards can be just as valuable and as regarded as the Grand Crus.

Since Pinot Noir is a thin-skinned grape that produces light-colored wines, there's a noticeable difference between wines that are aged and matured in oak barrels and those that aren't. On the whole, the best red Burgundy wines spend some time in oak, adding depth, flavor, and character.

Further south in Burgundy, Gamay produces wines in the appellation Beaujolais. Most of the wines from here are written off as cheap and easy plonk, but some excellent wines can be found.

*Vineyards in Beaujolais in southern Burgundy, France.*

More than 1,000 years ago, Cabernet Franc was first planted at the abbey of Bourgueil where it is still cultivated today.

---

The following producers all make different styles of reds from the Rhône Valley; some are soft and approachable; others are collectable wines that need years to mellow.

- Guigal
- René Rostaing
- Jean-Louis Chave
- Delas
- M. Chapoutier
- Jaboulet

## Loire Valley

The Loire Valley's main black grape variety is Cabernet Franc. Considered to be one of the most difficult grapes to grow, it is fickle in the vineyard and requires a long, cool growing season with minimal rain. The Loire Valley is one of the few places where this occurs and where winemakers have the patience and fortitude for taming the vine. The best appellations for Cabernet France, or Breton as the grape is locally called, are Chinon, Bourgeuil, and Saumur-Champigny. When grown in the famous tufa soil, a dense white compressed fossil-chalk, the wines are bracingly firm with powerful aromas of herbs and red fruits. When grown in gravel and sand closer to the river, the wines are lighter and aromatic. For the Cabernet Franc enthusiast who prefers earthy, grungy, and pleasantly stinky wines, Chinon can't be missed.

Some fine red wines are also produced in Sancerre from Pinot Noir. Typically light to medium bodied with fresh aromas of raspberries and subtle pepper notes, they are usually priced lower than similar quality wines from further east in Burgundy.

Other red wines from the Loire Valley are produced from Gamay, Cot (Malbec), and Grolleau.

## Rhône Valley

Syrah and Grenache are the two main black varieties of the Rhône Valley in eastern France. Any producer in the world who grows either Syrah or Grenache always focuses on the reds from this valley, where Syrah and Grenache produce wines of unparalleled power, depth, and intrigue.

The Rhône Valley is made up of two halves. The northern half, or *Rhône Septentrionale*, is a narrow strip of land where vineyards hug the river and the appellations run from north to south. The southern half, *Rhône Méridionale*, is flatter and the vineyards are more spread out. Each half is incredibly unique—climatically, culturally, and viticulturally.

In the northern half, Syrah reigns supreme. The appellations of Hermitage, Crozes-Hermitage, Cornas, Côte-Rôtie, and St-Joseph produce the best Syrah wines. In most appellations, winemakers are permitted to add small amounts of white wine to the finished blend to cut the harsh and bitter tannins found in Syrah grapes. Some opt to do so; others refrain. Syrah wines from these appellations are powerful, gripping, intense, smoky, and robust.

*The village of Chinon on the banks of the Loire Valley, France.*

---

*In 1309 Pope Clement V moved his court from Rome to Avignon, thus placing the center of the Christian Empire in southern Rhône. His successor, Pope John XXII, planted vineyards around the summer papal palace Châteauneuf-du-Pape. Although the Roman Catholic popes left the area in 1378, Châteauneuf-du-Pape remained the property of the papacy until 1791. As a reference to this historic period, some wine bottles from this appellation are emblazoned with the Papal crest.*

Wines from the southern half of the valley are made from a blend of grapes. Grenache and Syrah are the base grapes, and Mourvèdre, Cinsault, and Carignan are used in smaller amounts. Regardless of the blend, the reds from the appellations of Gigondas, Vacqueyras, Reasteau, Lirac, and Châteauneuf-du-Pape are generally riper, richer, and have more alcohol than wines from the north.

Châteauneuf-du-Pape, the most famous appellation in the southern half, is a small zone when compared to some of the others, but it has two unique characteristics. The first is the soil, which is composed of round and sleek stones called *galets*. Resembling the stones used for massage therapy, they retain solar energy and help warm the vines into the evening as the sun wanes. They also reflect the sunshine throughout the day back onto the vine's leaves and berries. This appellation's other distinguishing factor is the selection of thirteen varieties of grapes that can be used to make wine. Producers such as Château de Beaucastel use all thirteen grapes, while others opt for only one grape, usually Grenache.

Further south in Languedoc-Roussillon and Provence, grapes like Grenache, Syrah, and Cinsault are the most popular. Although less known, wines from these areas can rival the reds from further north in the Rhône Valley.

*The sloping hills of Barolo are as unique as the wines that are born here.*

# Italy

Red wines from Tuscany and Piedmont are the most popular and expensive Italian reds, but each of Italy's twenty regions produce quality reds. With hundreds of indigenous grapes, the selection is endless. Whether grown in the mountain peaks of the north, the scenic hills and valleys of central Italy, or on the slopes of dormant volcanoes in the south, the reds of Italy are captivating.

## *Northwest*

The Piedmont is Italy's premier zone for red wines. Wines from Barolo and Barbaresco are produced entirely from Nebbiolo, an indigenous grape similar to Pinot Noir. Both grapes have thin skins but are loaded with tannins and acidity. Nebbiolo-based wines require barrel maturation for a few years to mellow out the harsh tannic grip. In their infancy Nebbiolo wines are light in color with strong notes of cranberry, herbs, and mushrooms. Over time the wines develop complex aromas and flavors of truffles, leather, tar, and forest herbs. As winemaker Danilo Drocco correctly states, "Barolo should reveal itself little by little, rather than all at once."

Barolos can age for decades—and even after years of slumbering, the wines are still powerful. Critics say that an older vintage bottle of Barolo is like "an iron fist in a velvet glove." Barbera, Dolcetto, Grignolino, and Freisa are other black grape varieties that are better enjoyed in their youth.

The Valle d'Aosta is known for reds produced from Nebbiolo (locally called Picotendro), Pinot Noir, Fumin, and Petit Rouge. Due to the high elevation of the vineyards, most wines are light in color with a soft floral flavor.

Liguria doesn't produce much red, but there are some bottles of Dolcetto (Ormeasco) and Grenache that are tasty.

Lombardia is the next best place for Nebbiolo outside of the Piedmont. All wines from the Valtellina appellation are produced almost exclusively from Nebbiolo (locally called Chiavenasca). Lacking the mushroom and funk of Piedmont Nebbiolo wines, they exhibit much more flinty, chalky, and mineral notes—due to the limestone and glacial soil near the border with Switzerland where the vines grow.

*Walls constructed out of aging Barolo in the cellars of Giacomo Borgogno e Figli. The cellar currently houses nearly 500,000 bottles of older vintages of Barolo that it's produced.*

*Barrels at Masi Agricola in Veneto.*

*Bottles of Amarone aging in the cellars of Masi Agricola.*

## Northeast

Some of the country's northernmost vineyards are in Trentino-Alto Adige. Lagrein is the region's most important indigenous grape, producing inky and dark colored wines with strong brambly fruit flavors. Cabernet, Merlot, and Pinot Noir are also grown to make wine.

The Veneto region is known for one of Italy's most popular wines, Amarone della Valpolicella, which is made from dried grapes, mostly Corvina. As the grapes shrivel, the water evaporates and the sugars concentrate. The finished wines are high in alcohol, which is offset by a bitter and tannic finish. Aromas of prunes, toffee, chocolate, and spice give way to silky raisinated fruit flavors. Some are best enjoyed in their youth, while others are meant for aging. They're excellent with hearty meat dishes and hard intense cheeses. Other wines from the area are simply called "Valpolicella" and are made using the same grapes, minus the drying process. They're usually light to medium in color and soft and fruity.

Further east, Friuli produces wines from Refosco, Pignolo, and Schioppettino indigenous grapes, in addition to the international varieties Cabernet Sauvignon, Merlot, and Cabernet Franc.

## Central Italy

Perhaps no other region in Italy is as enchanting and magical as Tuscany. The main grape of Tuscany—and all of central Italy—is Sangiovese, the base grape in many of the appellations in the region, including Brunello di Montalcino, Chianti, Morellino di Scansano, Vino Nobile di Montepulciano, and Carmignano. Most wines are light in color with flavors of cherries and red fruits mixed with leather and balsamic notes. In Montalcino, the grape is referred to as Brunello, and it is widely agreed that the best Sangiovese wines come from this sleepy hilltop town in southern Tuscany. After a few years of aging, Brunello wines are best enjoyed with a classic Tuscan dish, Pappardelle al Cinghiale (pasta with wild boar ragú).

Sangiovese is also used in many blended wines throughout the region. While there are no rules regarding a "Super-Tuscan," many of them are produced by blending Sangiovese with other grapes such as Cabernet Sauvignon, Merlot, and Syrah.

Umbria's best reds are made using Sagrantino, an indigenous grape. The grape is loaded with pigments and polyphenols, and the wines are powerful, tannic, and gripping. Some producers also produce a wine called Montefalco Rosso, a blend of Sangiovese with Sagrantino. These wines are a bit more approachable and easier on the wallet.

On the eastern coast of central Italy in Le Marche, Sangiovese is blended with Montepulciano. Wines labeled Rosso Conero are blends of the two grapes. The wines incorporate the earthy and acidic nature of Sangiovese with the plump fruity and dark color of Montepulciano.

Montepulciano d'Abruzzo, one of the most popular Italian red wines, can come from anywhere within Abruzzo, and so there are many different styles of the wine. Most versions are medium- to full-bodied with soft blackberry and black cherry flavors. Some producers, such as Emidio Pepe, hone in on the uniqueness of the grape and produce age-worthy wines that that develop intense tobacco, spice, and black olive flavors over time.

*The hilltop town of Montalcino in Southern Tuscany.*

*Sangiovese grapes in Montalcino at harvest time.*

*Tenuta Castelbuono's Carapace with Sagrantino vines in the autumn season.*

## Southern Italy

Campania is the best place for wines made from the Aglianico grape. While grown all over the southern portion of Italy, the grape achieves its best expression in the Taurasi appellation. The wines are light to medium in color and in certain years can rival the best Barolo wines. Since the soil is mostly volcanic bedrock, many of the wines exhibit charred and smoky aromas and flavors.

Puglia is one of Italy's flatter regions. Its scorching hot days are well suited for black-skinned grapes such as Primitivo and Negroamaro. Primitivo is genetically similar to Zinfandel, and the wines are similar in style—big, plump, and rich. The Salice Salentino appellation is one of Puglia's best. Red wines are based on Negroamaro with a small addition of Malvasia Nera, another indigenous grape. The wines are fruity and supple.

Calabria is at the southern end of the mainland. Its best appellation is Ciró, located on the eastern coast. Wines are made using the native grape Gaglioppo and are usually light and aromatic with easygoing cherry fruit flavors.

## Islands

Sicily is one of the most productive regions in all of Italy, and its wineries sell a good amount of wine in bulk to producers in other countries, who use it for blending purposes. A lot of this wine is made using the Nero d'Avola grape. Like Montepulciano in Abruzzo, Nero d'Avola is grown all over Sicily. Stylistically, the grape produces wines that go from light, dry, and simple to heavy, rich, and powerful. It all depends on where the wine is produced and how it is aged. Grapes such as Cabernet Sauvignon, Merlot, and Syrah also grow well in Sicily's hot and dry climate. In the east, Nerello Mascalese and Nerello Capuccio, both native grapes, are grown on the slopes of Mount Etna. The wines are popular with consumers who like light- to medium-bodied wines with earthy, smoky, and pungent aromas. In southeastern Sicily Nero d'Avola is blended with Frappato to produce Cerasuolo di Vittoria. They're some of Sicily's most food-friendly and approachable wines.

Italy's other large island, Sardinia, produces a wide variety of wines. Grapes like Monica, Bovale Sardo, Carignano, and Cannonau (Grenache) are most popular. Many vineyard managers grow other crops and herbs alongside the vineyards, and the wines usually have some vegetal and herbaceous aromas.

*Seaside vineyards at La Foresteria, part of the Planeta family of wineries in Sicily.*

# Spain

Spain's most important black variety, Tempranillo is the dominant grape variety in Spain's most prestigious zones. In Rioja, the grape is blended with Mazuelo (Carignan), Graciano, and Garnacha, along with a few others such as Cabernet Sauvignon and Monastrel.

There are theories that Tempranillo is related to Pinot Noir. Although wines from the two grapes share similar finesse and elegance, Tempranillo is lower in natural acids and blends well with other grapes, whereas Pinot is best expressed on its own.

Rioja, Spain's premier wine zone for reds, has three sub-regions: Rioja Alavesa, Rioja Baja, and Rioja Alta. Some producers blend grapes from all three zones to make well-rounded blends, while other producers prefer using grapes from just one sub-region.

Castilla y León is a large region in the northern central part of the country. The principle red wine zone in this region is Ribera del Duero. Tempranillo, locally referred to as Tinto del País, is produced as a varietal-wine and is also blended with Cabernet Sauvignon, Merlot, Malbec, and Garnacha. Other appellations that incorporate Tempranillo are Toro and Cigales. Mencía, another indigenous grape, is showcased in Bierzo.

Further east in Cataluña, Garnacha and Cariñena are the main grapes used to make the famous reds in the Priorat appellation. The wines are big, tannic, and powerful, usually needing years of aging before they can be enjoyed. Llicorella, the famous soil where these vines grow, is a mix of black slate and quartz that requires the vines to dig deep into the bedrock in search of water.

In southern Spain, the Monastrel grape is planted in some of the hottest, driest, and highest elevation spots in the country. The wines are powerful, intense, and brooding with rich fruit flavors and tannic finishes. Other grapes that grow well here are Cabernet Sauvignon and Syrah.

*Opposite page: White grapes at harvest in the limestone-rich soil of southern Spain.*

*Tempranillo takes on different names throughout the country.*

- *Toro: Tinta del Toro*
- *Cataluña: Ull de Llebre*
- *Castilla La Mancha: Cencibel*
- *Castilla y León: Tinto Fino, or Tina del País*

---

*Spain is one of the European countries that favors American oak barrels for maturing its wines. The results are aromas of coconut, dill, and lanolin. French oak, on the other hand, tends to impart stronger aromas of vanilla and cream.*

---

*Half of the European Union's vineyards are in Spain, almost three million acres (1,214,056 hectares). But this doesn't mean that Spain produces half of the wine. In fact, the yields in Spain are much lower than most other countries. Why? Not all the vines are used for wine; the vines are not as densely planted; and not all the vines are as productive as they are in other countries.*

# Portugal

Madeira and port are the foundation of the Portuguese wine industry, but there are more than 200 indigenous grape varieties that today's producers are hoping will produce wines that cater to global preferences. Touriga Nacional, also called Bical and Mortágua Preto, is the cherished variety for port. When it is not used for fortified wines, the grape produces inky, full-bodied reds with plump fruit. Alfrocheiro, Trincadeira (Tinta Amarela), Baga (the country's most widely planted black grape), and Aragonez are other widely cultivated, promising black grapes.

In north central Portugal, Dão, with its warm summers and sandy, gravel soil was one of the first areas recognized by the government as a classified growing area. Regulations stipulate that at least 20 percent of the Touriga Nacional grape must be used in all wines. Other grapes include Bastardo, Tinto Pinheira, and Tinta Roriz (Tempranillo). Some consumers feel that Dão is past its prime and the country's eager producers should look elsewhere for future growth, but loyalists believe its best days are yet ahead. The Duoro Valley in the north is port country, but the vast improvement of dry red wines are enhancing the image of the entire country.

# Germany

Most of the red wine produced in Germany is made from Pinot Noir, locally referred to as Spätburgunder. Other grapes include Blauer Portugieser, Trollinger, and Dornfelder. The small region of Arh in the northwest is devoted to red wines. Almost nine out of ten vineyards are planted to black varieties. Most wines are light in color with red and garnet hues and are soft and approachable. When aged in oak, they can take on darker and more powerful profiles.

*Terraced vineyards in the Duoro River Valley in Portugal.*

# Austria

Many of Austria's red wines are produced from indigenous grapes: Zweigelt, Blaufränkisch, St. Laurent, Blauer Portugieser, and Blauburger. International varieties such as Pinot Noir are also cultivated. The best reds come from the very east of the country in Burgenland. This area borders Hungary and the temperatures in the summer are the hottest in the country. Many of the black-skinned grapes that grow here are low in tannins and color pigments, resulting in light, quaffy, and aromatic reds. Many of these are aged in oak barrels, even if only for a brief amount of time, to add some color and body to the wines.

# Bulgaria

Bulgaria has had a tumultuous history of wine production, and some vineyards in prime spots have either been abandoned altogether or mismanaged due to political strife and European economic woes. Vineyards are at the same latitude as central Italy, southern France, and northern Spain, and the climate is an ideal one for growing grapes. Cabernet Sauvignon and Merlot are the most popular grapes planted, but indigenous grapes like Mavrud and Gamza may hold the key to Bulgaria's success in the long run.

# Romania

Romania, the fifth largest producer of wine in Europe, has eight wine regions and more than thirty-five smaller districts. The Black Sea helps mitigate the vast day and night temperatures. Pinot Noir is considered to be Romania's calling card, but Merlot and Cabernet Sauvignon are also grown and produce pleasant and fruity reds.

*The Rhine River was the northern boundary of the Roman Empire, and Christian monks there spread the knowledge of vine growing and winemaking to most of Germany.*

*Vienna, Austria is the only European capital to have a government-recognized wine zone within its city borders.*

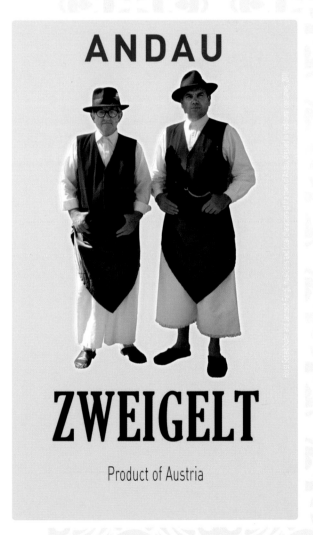

# New World Red Wines

## United States

### California

California's countryside is a vast spread of rolling hills and valleys with numerous mountain ranges running parallel to the coastline. These ridges create pockets of fog and help grapevines survive the long and hot summers. They also block treacherous winds and rains coming off the Pacific. Inland rivers and lakes such as the Napa River, Carneros Creek, and Lake Hennessey also moderate temperatures throughout the year.

California red wine begins with Cabernet Sauvignon. The wines are medium- to full-bodied with strong aromas of ripe blackberries and dark brambly fruits. Most everyday wines are easy-going and plump, with noticeable vanilla notes from French barrel maturation. Top-notch and collectable Cabernets are more tannic in their youth. As they age they develop intense aromas of figs, dried fruits, herbs, and mushrooms.

### North Coast

Napa County encompasses all the vineyards within the Napa Valley, the United States' most famous wine zone. Although the valley is small, about 30 miles (48 km) long and 5 miles (8 km) across at its widest point, hundreds of small producers specialize in different varieties. Many of the vineyards are on the valley floor or at the base of the surrounding hills, nestled between the Mayacamas Mountains and the Coast Range. Cabernet Sauvignon leads the way in prestige, but excellent wines are also produced from Zinfandel, Merlot, Syrah, and Petite Sirah.

*The Townsend Vineyard of Antica Winery in Atlas Peak, Napa Valley.*

The major AVAs within the Napa Valley are divided between the valley floor and the slopes of the mountains.

| Valley Floor AVAs | Mountain AVAs |
|---|---|
| Calistoga | Mayacamas Range |
| St. Helena | Diamond Mountain |
| Rutherford | Spring Mountain |
| Oakville | Mount Veeder |
| Yountville | Howell Mountain |
| Stag's Leap | Atlas Peak |
| Oak Knoll | Chiles Valley District |
| Los Carneros | |
| (shared with | |
| Sonoma County) | |
| Wild Horse Valley | |

Rutherford, Oakville, and Yountville are considered the top places for Cabernet Sauvignon. Many of the country's most prized wines are produced from vineyards within these zones.

Northwest of Napa County, Sonoma County also has numerous small AVAs. The San Pablo Bay cools the southern sections of the county where grapes such as Pinot Noir are grown. Further north, warmer climate grapes such as Cabernet Sauvignon and Zinfandel are popular. Sonoma Coast is Somona County's largest appellation, stretching north to south on the western side of the county. Within this appellation are smaller zones such as Chalk Hill, Green Valley, Carneros, Sonoma Valley, and Russian River Valley, each with its own "meso-climate." Seek out wines from Sonoma-Cutrer, Flowers, Hartford Court, and Kistler.

While wines from Mendocino and Lake Counties aren't as well known as those from Sonoma and Napa, many are just as exciting and delicious. The more popular grapes are Cabernet Sauvignon, Petite Sirah, Merlot, and Zinfandel. Look for wines from the Anderson Valley, Mendocino Ridge, and Redwood Valley appellations in Mendocino and from Clear Lake, Benmore, and Guenoc Valley appellations in Lake County.

*Since 1961, Cabernet Sauvignon plantings have risen from 600 acres (242 hectares) to more than 90,000 (36,421 hectares).*

*Meritage wines are a blend of two or more different grapes that model a Bordeaux wine. For reds, the grapes include Cabernet Sauvignon, Merlot, Cabernet Franc, Malbec, and Petit Verdot. For whites, the grapes include Sauvignon Blanc, Semillon, and Muscadelle. With production capped at 25,000 cases per vintage, Meritage wines must be labeled as "the best wine of its type produced by the winery." Many wine lists have a "Meritage" or "Blended Wine" category to delineate these French-inspired wines from the rest of American wines.*

*Some of Sonoma County's major growing areas are:*

- *Dry Creek Valley*
- *Alexander Valley*
- *Knights Valley*
- *Russian River Valley*
- *Chalk Hill*
- *Green Valley*
- *Los Carneros (shared with Napa)*

## Central Coast

South of San Francisco, the rugged Santa Cruz Mountains provide only patches of vineyard space, so producing quality wine here requires both intuition and grit. Some of California's best producers are located in this part of the state, such as Calera, Chalone, Rosenblum, and Jekel Vineyard. The aging potential of Ridge Vineyards' reds have silenced critics who say California is unable to produce red wines intended for the long haul. Whether Cabernet Sauvignon or Zinfandel, Ridge Vineyards wines are worth exploring.

Further south, Zinfandel has staked its claim as the leading grape of Paso Robles. The wines are big and structured, with potent aromas of blackberries, spices, and high alcohol levels. Other grapes grown are Petit Sirah, Syrah, and Cabernet Sauvignon. Pinot Noir is the darling grape of Santa Barbara, where the cool climate provides a long and gradual growing season. Wines from the Bien Nacido Vineyard in the Santa Maria Valley and the Sanford and Benedict Vineyard in the Santa Ynez Valley are considered top-notch expressions of American Pinot Noir.

Many farmers own small parcels in these vineyards, so it is common to see the name of one specific vineyard on different producers' wine labels. Trying these wines, especially ones from the same vintage, is a great way to taste the best of California's Pinot Noirs and decide for yourself which producers you favor. Some wines are light and aromatic; others are bigger and more structured, resulting from extended oak maturation.

Due to the rising success of California wine, many European winemakers have ventured to California to expand their horizons.

Here are some of the more famous California properties with European ownership:

**Opus One** – Located in Oakville within the Napa Valley. The winery is a joint venture between the Mondavi family and Baron Philippe de Rothschild of Bordeaux fame. First vintage: 1979.

**Dominus Estate** – Located in Yountville within the Napa Valley. Co-founded by Christian Moueix, the owner of Château Pétrus in Bordeaux, France. First vintage: 1984.

**Roederer Estate** – Located in Anderson Valley within Mendocino. Founded by the Champagne house of Roederer. First vintage: 1994.

**Domaine Carneros** – Located in Los Carneros within the Napa Valley. The winery is a joint venture between the Champagne house Taittinger and Kobrand, its distribution and marketing partner. First vintage: 1989.

**Antica** – Located in Atlas Peak within the Napa Valley. Founded by Marchese Piero Antinori, the patriarch of Tuscany's Antinori winemaking family. First vintage: 2004.

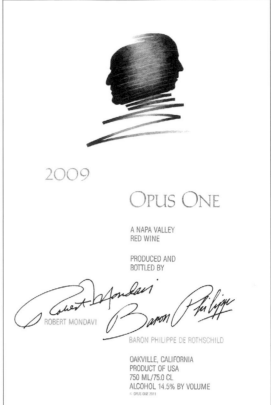

2009

OPUS ONE

A NAPA VALLEY
RED WINE

PRODUCED AND
BOTTLED BY

ROBERT MONDAVI

BARON PHILIPPE DE ROTHSCHILD

OAKVILLE, CALIFORNIA
PRODUCT OF USA
750 ML/75.0 CL
ALCOHOL 14.5% BY VOLUME

*The Opus One Winery in Oakville, Napa Valley.*

## Oregon

Other than Santa Barbara and pockets of Sonoma, Oregon is Pinot Noir country for the United States. Other varieties include Syrah, Cabernet Sauvignon, Merlot, and Maréchal Foch, a French hybrid that grows well in cool climates.

Winemaking dates to the 1850s in Oregon, but until recently the state relied heavily on indigenous grapes such as Concord. Conditions officially changed for the better in the 1960s when producers began to take Oregon's soil and climate more seriously. HillCrest, established in 1961 by Richard Sommer in the Umpqua Valley, was the first winery to make a serious impact. Although overshadowed by the results and impact of the 1976 "Judgment of Paris," Oregon has also fared well in a 1979 international comparison tasting. David Lett's 1975 Eyrie Vineyards Pinot Noir from Oregon placed second in a blind tasting of more than 600 different Burgundian-style Pinot Noir wines from around the world. From this point on, Oregon was viewed as a viable place to grow Pinot Noir. As in California, many successful European winemakers have since set up shop in Oregon.

Oregon and Burgundy, France, share many geographic similarities. Most importantly, they are both located at the 45th parallel and are nestled between mountain ranges, which create cooler climates and longer, gradual growing seasons. The light-colored wines eloquently showcase Pinot Noir's trademark mix of rosy, mushroom aromas and ripe red berry fruits.

A large portion of Oregon's reds come from the Willamette Valley, a large 50-mile (80-km) parcel of land running from Portland in the north to Eugene in the south and flanked by the Cascade Range in the east and the Coast Range in the west. The best vineyards receive the benefits of the nearby Willamette River. Like California's top regions, there are large fluctuations in the temperature throughout the day—conditions that promote high-quality grapes, culminating in high-quality wines.

*Oregon has more than 450 wineries and more than 20,000 acres (8,093 hectares) of vineyards, the majority of which are planted to Pinot Noir.*

***Opposite page:*** *Remnants of pruning the vines prior to spring.*

Bethel Heights
VINEYARD

2009
PINOT NOIR

Willamette Valley

## Washington

Outside of California, Washington State produces the most wine in the United States. There are more than 750 wineries, most of which are located east of the Cascade Mountains throughout the state's thirteen AVAs. Due to the terrain, many parts of Washington receive more sunlight than California, making it ideal for black varieties such as Cabernet Sauvignon, Merlot, Syrah, Cabernet Franc, and Malbec. Columbia Valley, the state's largest appellation, has smaller and more specific appellations located within its borders. The average rainfall is between 8 and 10 inches (20 to 25 cm) per year, and the temperature change between night and day is extreme—perfect conditions for grapevines. Some great wines have been made from all the aforementioned grapes, but there has been momentum behind Syrah. As Oregon has taken to Pinot Noir, Washington's wineries are hoping that Syrah will give the state a better global identity.

The Yakima Valley, a sub-district of the Columbia Valley, accounts for nearly half of the state's wineries. The state's first approved AVA, it is generally considered the home of Washington State wine. Advocates are excited for the future, because grapevines are beginning to supplant the apple trees that take up the better real estate, relics from the massive plantings dating to President Franklin D. Roosevelt's New Deal.

*A recent addition to Washington's AVA roster is Naches Heights, located within the greater Columbia Valley. Registered in 2012, it is the state's first sustainable AVA—all seven vineyards are practicing organic, sustainable, and/or biodynamic farming.*

---

*The first* vinifera *grapevine in Washington was planted in 1871 in the Yakima Valley.*

*Vineyard in Yakima County, Washington, during summer growing season.*

*In 1976, New York passed the Farm Winery Act. It helped create many family farm wineries that remain a large part of the wine community today. Other states followed suit and created their own versions of the act to promote the growth of wine producing.*

## New York

Four major wine zones exist in New York: Lake Erie, Finger Lakes, Hudson Valley, and Long Island. Within each zone are smaller AVAs that specialize in certain grapes. On Long Island, about 50 wineries produce wines on a small scale and are equipped with tasting rooms and event spaces designed to cater to metropolitans looking for a weekend getaway. The climate is cool and damp, and the specialty wines are produced from Cabernet Franc, Merlot, and Cabernet Sauvignon.

Cayuga, a small appellation within the larger encompassing Finger Lakes appellation in the northern part of the state, is slightly warmer and the hillsides provide excellent drainage and exposure to the sun. It is a young and budding environment for New York wines, but the future looks bright. New York City is America's stage for the culinary arts, and local wines will always have a place on the table.

NORTH FORK OF
LONG ISLAND

M E R L O T

UNFILTERED

Hudson Valley vineyards abut the Hudson River as it runs from Albany south towards New York City. Cool-climate grapes such as Cabernet Franc and Pinot Noir grow best here. Nestled within the valley is the country's oldest vineyard, Benmarl, planted in the early 1800s. Brotherhood Winery, founded in 1839, is the country's oldest continuously-operating winery.

Lake Erie vineyards are mostly planted to Concord grapes, which are used to make grape juice and jam.

## Other States

Here are some important wine-producing states and the red wines they focus on.

| State | Grape |
| --- | --- |
| Connecticut | Pinot Noir, Cabernet Franc, Merlot, Chancellor |
| Indiana | Cabernet Sauvignon, Catawba |
| Maryland | Chambourcin, Cabernet Sauvignon, Merlot |
| Massachusetts | Maréchel Foch, Cabernet Sauvignon, Pinot Noir, Merlot |
| Michigan | Concord, Cabernet Sauvignon, Merlot, Pinot Noir |
| New Hampshire | Cabernet Franc, Noiret, Maréchel Foch, Chambourcin, Merlot, Malbec, Carmenère |
| New Jersey | Chambourcin, Chancellor, Cabernet Sauvignon, Merlot, Maréchel Foch, Pinot Noir, Leon Millet |
| New Mexico | Cabernet Sauvignon, Pinot Noir, Merlot, Zinfandel, Malbec, Dolcetto |
| Ohio | Catawba, Concord, Cabernet Sauvignon, Cabernet France, Pinot Noir, Merlot |
| Pennsylvania | Chambourcin, Cabernet Franc, Merlot, Cabernet Sauvignon, Pinot Noir |
| Rhode Island | Maréchel Foch, Cabernet Sauvignon, Cabernet Franc, Merlot, Pinot Noir |
| Texas | Cabernet Sauvignon, Cabernet Franc, Merlot, Pinot Noir, Ruby Cabernet, Chambourcin, Chancellor |
| Virginia | Chambourcin, Cabernet Sauvignon, Cabernet Franc, Merlot, Pinot Noir, Barbera |

# Canada

The first commercial wine in Canada was made in 1866 on Peele Island, and by the end of the century there were nearly 50 wineries. Growth was slow for Canada from that point on. The cool temperatures make it difficult to grow grapevines year round, except only in certain areas. Ontario and British Columbia are the two major wine-producing zones. Within each province, there are smaller Designated Viticultural Areas (DVAs), where most of Canada's quality wine is made. Cool climate grapes like Pinot Noir and Cabernet Franc make some of the country's best reds.

*Look for wines from the esteemed properties of Catena, Susana Balbo's Dominio del Plata, Bressia, and Achával Ferrer.*

---

*The average Argentinean consumes almost 150 pounds of beef per year. All that meat needs a glass of red to go with it. It is no surprise that three-fourths of Argentinean wine is consumed domestically.*

---

*Malbec, indigenous to France, has become Argentina's premiere grape. It fell out of favor in its native land after* phylloxera *decimated European vineyards. The vine became less productive and less reliable when grafted to American rootstock. In Argentina, however, the soil has a sandy composition, which fends off* phylloxera *and other louse and fungal diseases. Most of the grapevines are planted with the natural rootstock of the vine and not grafted.*

# Argentina

Argentina is the only major wine-producing country that doesn't have a large body of water near its most important vineyards. Instead, Argentina's growers take advantage of the massive Andes Mountains to regulate the temperature in their vineyards. They also use the mountains' runoff water for irrigation. Because the mountains block a lot of rain that comes from the West, Argentina has a hot and extremely dry climate.

The country ranks sixth in global wine production, much of which is produced from Malbec. The recent arrival of Argentina on the global wine stage is due in large part to a decline in domestic consumption. In 1970, the Argentinean consumption per person was 122 bottles of wine a year. Currently it is less than half this number. Despite the drop, only a quarter of the wine is exported. Vineyard plantings are skyrocketing and the sea of Argentinean wine is only growing.

From north to south, Argentina's three main wine zones are the Northern Provinces, Cuyo, and Patagonia. Within these zones are a number of smaller regions, further divided into specific appellations. Salta, the primary appellation in the Northern Provinces, has less than 10,000 acres (4,000 hectares) and a strong emphasis on black grapes such as Malbec and Cabernet Sauvignon.

Cuyo is the largest of the three main zones, and the smaller regions within Cuyo are the most important for wine, including La Rioja, Mendoza, and San Juan. Malbec from these areas are considered the best of what Argentina is capable of producing. The wines, oaked for a brief time, are brooding, heavy, and lush with mountain fruit flavors and rich, silky textures. Shiraz, Bonarda, Cabernet Sauvignon, Tannat, Merlot, and Petit Verdot are also cultivated throughout the country.

Patagonia is the southernmost area for wine production in Argentina. The cooler climate is better suited to grapes like Pinot Noir, which is becoming the premier grape. Founded by the Incisa delle Rochetta family of Italian winemaking fame, Bodegas Chacra has helped put Patagonia on the radar with its ultra-premium Pinot Noir wines.

# Chile

Chile has had strong ties to French winemakers since 1830 when Frenchman Claudio Gay created a botanical nursery devoted to botany and viticulture. Ever since, French winemakers have been involved in Chilean winemaking, leaving an indelible mark. Many of the grapes are of French origin, many of the winemaking techniques are French-inspired, and there's plenty of investment from French companies.

In the Aconcagua Valley, warm-climate grapes such as Cabernet Sauvignon, Merlot, and Syrah are the most popular. Producers closer to the coastline can successfully grow cool-climate grapes like Nebbiolo and Pinot Noir. Further south and closer to the capital of Santiago is the Maipo Valley. The average rainfall is only 12 inches per year, so many producers salvage the runoff water from the Andes and use it for irrigation throughout the year. Cabernet Sauvignon wines from this area are soft, supple, and silky with round and creamy black fruits.

*Viña Casa Marin in Chile*

One of the best things to happen to Chile was the discovery that many of the vineyards believed to be Merlot were in fact of another grape called Carmenère. The wines resemble Merlot in that they're soft and juicy with blueberry and blackberry currant flavors, but the widespread cultivation of Carmenère provides Chile with something that no other country can—a wide assortment of wines produced from this grape.

# Brazil

Rio Grande do Sul is the heart of Brazil's wine industry. The country's wine zones are in the south where temperatures are generally the coolest. The wines from Serra Gaúcha, a smaller area within Rio Grande, have emerged as some of the country's best. Its success has attracted interest from foreign winemakers, and there has been a surge of investment and more plantings. The world's leading enologists are also flocking to Brazil to investigate what Brazil has to offer.

The main black grape varieties are Pinot Noir, Cabernet Sauvignon, Merlot, Tannat, Ancellota, Egiodola, Tourigan Nacional, Tinta Roriz, and Marselan, a cross between Cabernet Sauvignon and Grenache. Cabernet Franc is also planted and is rapidly increasing in vineyard acreage.

# Uruguay

Uruguay is South America's fourth largest wine producer. Most wines are based on Tannat, a French grape. The wines are inky and full-bodied for the most part with dark brambly fruit flavors. Many of the country's leading wine producers are of European heritage, and their intentions and ambitions are of the same caliber as their brethren in Europe. In 1988, Uruguay created the Instituto Nacional de Viniviticultura, an initiative aimed at improving the quality and marketing of the country's wines.

*Vineyards along the coast of Chile.*

*Tannat – Uruguay's most important black variety.*

# Australia

Penfolds is one of the most important producers of Australian wine. In 1961, Penfolds Bin 61A placed first in a blind-tasting competition in Bordeaux. Its success helped open the doors for many other producers to enter the global market for quality table wines. The country has since earned a reputation for making value-priced wines produced from grapes like Shiraz (Syrah), Chardonnay, and Cabernet Sauvignon.

Riding the unprecedented modern-day success of Yellowtail, many producers began churning out like-minded wines, rich with fruit and offering extreme value. For a while, it seemed as if any grape could be grown and transformed into wine. Then, in an extreme case, Pinot Noir, which generally thrives in cooler climates, was unconscionably planted in the hot and dry Barossa Valley with disastrous results. Learning from past mistakes, the country's leading producers are looking to the cooler climates throughout Australia's sixty-five growing regions.

Changing the landscape of Australian wine are new vineyard sites at higher elevations and modified winemaking techniques. Shiraz producers are experimenting with different vineyard practices and

fermentation methods, such as whole-bunch fermentation, which gives the wines earthier and stemmy flavors. Wineries are also eschewing new oak and opting for larger and older barrels, yielding better fruit and oak tannin integration. These changes prompt Michael Hill Smith, one of Australia's leading wine personalities, to say that Australia's "best days are ahead."

The growth of Australia's wine industry in the last thirty years has been extraordinary. From 1982 through 2007, exports grew from 8 million liters to 805 million liters. Along the way, the country adopted a thirty-year initiative to become the "world's leading exporter of quality branded wines." The country is now the fourth largest exporting country, behind European behemoths France, Italy, and Spain. Its success has only fueled the fire for more growth and it is estimated that more than 12 acres (4 hectares) of Chardonnay are planted each day and a new winery is launched every eighty-four hours.

The major wine regions are located along the southern cost of the continent. They are further divided into smaller appellations, each offering its own specialties. While temperature and soil vary, dry conditions are common throughout the country, and irrigation is necessary in most places.

## South Australia

Coonawara, one of the southernmost regions in the country, usually has a late harvest. The soil is referred to as *terra rossa*, a red loam soil with high limestone content. Cabernet Sauvignon and Shiraz wines produced from vines that grow in this soil are some of the best Australian wines to be found. They're rich in color with intense flavors and great aging potential.

Barossa Valley is home to perhaps the most famous Australian wine of all: Grange, produced by Penfolds. First made in 1951, the wine is based on Shiraz with a splash of Cabernet Sauvignon. It resembles the great reds from Hermitage in the Rhône Valley of France. If such luxury isn't affordable, there are many other great Shiraz-based wines produced in Barossa Valley that offer up layers of fruit and have firm, gripping tannins. Eden Valley is home to the renowned Hill of Grace vineyard, where Shiraz vines more than 135 years old are used to make structured and powerful wines.

## Victoria

When gold was discovered in Australia in the 1850s, European immigrants flocked to Victoria and brought with them an insatiable thirst for wine. Vineyard plantings flourished and wine production commenced. When the gold ran dry, right about the time when *phylloxera* appeared, wine production ceased and vineyards were abandoned. It would be nearly one hundred years before grapes were replanted at Mount Mary vineyard in the Yarra Valley.

The smallest of all the mainland states, Victoria is second in total wine produced, behind South Australia. James Halliday, one of the country's most influential wine personalities, established Coldstream Hills Winery in 1985. Other winegrowers followed and the revival of former glory is underway in Victoria. Appellations like Rutherglen and King Valley are known for dessert wines, or "stickies," produced from Muscat and Muscadelle.

*Coonawarra – One of Australia's best places to grow Shiraz.*

## New South Wales

Hunter Valley, the most important appellation in New South Wales, produces many of Australia's most popular wines. The vineyards benefit from the coastal effects of the Tasman Sea, while its proximity to Sydney makes the appellation accessible to tourists. Shiraz, the leading grape variety, makes big and brash red wines with beefy and intense flavors. Viognier and Pinot Noir also grow well here. Other appellations include Mudgee, Orange, Cowra, Riverina, and one of Australia's coolest and most picturesque growing areas, Tumbarumba.

## Queensland and Northern Territory

The vineyards of Queensland and Northern Territory, to the north and east of the aforementioned regions, were once thought to be ill planted due to the area's extreme heat. Today wineries are discovering some good vineyard sites that are worth exploring. Grapes are grown in various climates, such as the high-altitude vineyards in Granite Belt, where the elevation reaches 3,100 feet (1,000 m). Cabernet Sauvignon, Chardonnay, and Shiraz lead the way. Given the obscurity of this area, wines can be hard to locate, but usually offer great value when found.

# New Zealand

With the end of World War II, soldiers returning home to New Zealand created a huge demand for alcohol. As a result, wine production skyrocketed. While the quality of wine generally increased, the rate of new vineyard plantings and wine production increased exponentially and an excess of wine quickly developed. To rectify this, in 1985 the government purchased nearly 3,000 acres (1,214 hectares) of vineyards and ripped up many of the vines in an effort to stabilize future supply. The country quickly learned from its mistakes and has become a reliable source for interesting and new expressions of classic grape varieties.

*Waikato and Bay of Plenty are two other appellations in North Island. Mostly farmland used for livestock grazing, the regions have only fifteen commercial wineries. Cabernet Sauvignon and Merlot are the preferred grapes.*

*Vineyards on South Island of New Zealand.*

Created in 1996, New Zealand's appellation system is rather lax as producers aren't bound to the same rigidity as those in European countries, specifically regarding grape varieties. Critics denigrate the system for its vagaries as to geographic boundaries and inconsistent labeling legislation.

Many of the country's 700 wineries are small, family-run properties. Roughly 90 percent produce less than 20,000 cases annually, creating a diverse selection of wines that are different confirmations of the country's growing potential. Total production is about twenty-two million cases per wine, and more than two-thirds of production is exported, principally to the United Kingdom, the United States, and Australia.

Central Otago has emerged as the most reputable source for New Zealand Pinot Noir. The region, considered by many as the world's most southerly growing region, is conveniently nestled in the shadow of the Southern Alps. On the western side of the mountains, the rainfall averages nearly 300 inches (760 cm) of rain per year, while in Central Otago the average precipitation is 15 inches (38 cm) per year. This causes the roots of the vines to dig deep into the ground for water, strengthening the vine itself and producing more mature and quality grapes. The conditions are also dry and cool throughout the year, ideal for Pinot Noir. With a latitude of nearly 45° south, snowcapped mountain ranges and glaciers provide a backdrop for vineyard managers strolling the rows. This landscape would be the equivalent to glaciers in Oregon, which is located at roughly 45° north latitude.

Heightened levels of UV rays offset the cooler temperatures of southern New Zealand, stimulating vine growth and energizing plant development. The intense exposure to the sun can be detrimental to the grapes, however. Many vineyard managers use the leaves as a protective canopy for the grapes, positioning the leaves and shoots to shield the grapes from the scorching afternoon rays.

## North Island

Northland, home to some of New Zealand's first attempts at winemaking, has only sixteen commercial wineries, most growing warmer climate grapes such as Cabernet Sauvignon, Merlot, and Syrah. While some wines from the area are good, the humidity and warmth make it difficult to manage the vines throughout the year.

Merlot, the most widely-planted black grape in Hawke's Bay, produces structured and full-bodied wines. Hawke's Bay is generally warm and the growing season is longer, with the most hours of sun in the country. The loose soil provides good drainage for the vines. More than 70 percent of the 150-plus wineries actively participate in the Sustainable Winegrowing New Zealand movement.

*Felton Road Winery, one of New Zealand's best wineries.*

## South Island

Canterbury and Waipara are two of the larger winemaking zones, with Chardonnay and Pinot Noir accounting for 60 percent of all vineyard plantings. The average annual rainfall is around 25 inches (63 cm), and the autumn season is cooler than elsewhere on the island. Most of the vineyards are planted in the alluvial plains and valley floors, yielding light- to medium-bodied wines with fresh aromatic profiles.

Central Otago is the most significant place for red wines on the South Island, perhaps in the whole country. Hillside vineyard plantings are essential in this part of the island so solar energy can help the vines grow and stave off frost in the spring and autumn seasons. Deciding which grapes to grow in this difficult climate was anybody's guess until recently. While most growers played it safe by using German white varieties, which were proven to provide good yields in cool climates, others looked to Pinot Noir and other red grapes. Since then, Pinot Noir has become the grape of choice, accounting for more than 80 percent of all vineyards.

Since it is in the rain shadow of the Southern Alps, the climate is generally dry, which allows growers to bypass the chemicals associated with fending off rot and fungus caused by reoccurring humidity. The Pinot Noir wines are silky and very fragrant, with mushroom and raspberry aromas. Wines of balance, they're now included in the conversation when discussing the red wines of Burgundy, France.

# South Africa

Almost all of South Africa's vineyards are within 100 miles (161 km) of Capetown. Stellenbosch and Paarl are its best wine districts. While South Africa has a lot to offer, the most important grape is Pinotage, a cross between Pinot Noir and Cinsaut. Consumers are either ardent fans of wines from Pinotage or they're vehemently against them; few people take the middle ground. While the wines are tasty enough, they are less exciting than Pinot Noir wines. Since not many plantings of the grape exist outside of South Africa, the grape's future as a popular variety rests with South Africa's vintners. Pinot Noir, Cabernet Sauvignon, Cabernet Franc, Merlot, and Shiraz are also planted.

South Africa has three main wine-growing regions: Coastal Region, Boberg Region, and Breede River Valley Region. Within these areas are smaller districts, further divided into wards (similar to appellations). Stellenbosch, in the Coastal Region, is considered the best place to make wine. Swartland and Cape Point are other districts where the quality of wine is increasing. Paarl is northeast of Stellenbosch and is known for Shiraz.

Other wine-growing regions are popping up, and producers are searching for the best land where hot meets cold, inevitably leading to quality grapes and eventually to complex and delicious wine. Producers in Klein Karoo and Olifants River are making some exciting wines worth seeking out.

# Other African Countries

In the first half of the century **Algeria** was a major country in the international wine market. At the height of its reign the country had nearly one million acres (404,685 hectares) of vineyards. Less than half exist today. With more than 75 percent of all vineyards older than forty years, quality grapes are readily available. Red wines worth trying are produced from Cinsault, Grenache, and Carignan.

**Morocco** and **Tunisia** were once thriving wine countries, but were stifled under Muslim rule. Within the last one hundred years, both countries have benefited from cultural and historical connections with France and the rest of Europe. Many of the best wines are based on Carignan, Cinsault, and Cabernet Sauvignon.

# China

China is one of the leading candidates to become a global leader in wine production, and many foreign companies are investing in its future. Wines from the Ningxia, Shaanxi, and Shandong Provinces are worth trying, although some of the Cabernet Sauvignon and Merlot wines are disappointing. China still needs to learn which grapes to grow in certain locations. Hopefully some indigenous grapes from China will rise up and bring significance to the country's wine movement. Until then, many of its new producers are relying on Cabernet Sauvignon and Merlot.

Look for wines from the following wards
of Stellenbosch:

- *Jonkershock Valley*
- *Simonsberg-Stellenbosch*
- *Bottelary*
- *Devon Valley*
- *Papgaaiberg*

———

*Some of Tunisia's vineyards are located
further north than Sicily's.*

*Champagne vineyards near Verzenay within the Montagne de Reims.*

# Old World Sparkling Wines

## France

The world's best sparkling wines are produced in the northern reaches of France, east of Paris, in the Champagne region. Located at the 48th parallel, Champagne is a challenging place to grow grapes. Cool temperatures, spring frosts, and autumn hailstorms are just a few of the obstacles with which farmers are faced. Ideally, sparkling wines are made from grapes high in acids, resulting in crisp, fresh, balanced wines. If plump, overly ripe grapes are used, the finished wine will lack elegance and minerality. Thus, cool climates like Champagne are ideal.

The three main varieties used in Champagne are Chardonnay, Pinot Noir, and Pinot Meunier. Although Pinot Noir and Pinot Meunier are red varieties, they're usually used to make white sparkling wine. This is made possible by separating the juice from the crushed skins at harvest time.

Many producers blend wines from one or two or sometimes all three grapes. Each grape brings certain characteristics to the finished wine. Chardonnay gives the wines elegance and finesse. Pinot Noir provides structure, body, and power. Pinot Meunier contributes fruitiness, youthfulness, and approachability. On average, Pinot Meunier and Pinot Noir comprise 60 to 70 percent of the blend and the remainder is Chardonnay.

Wines labeled "Blanc de Blanc" are produced entirely from Chardonnay and wines labeled "Blanc de Noir" are produced exclusively from obtaining the clear juice from the black grapes. Although the name suggests they're completely white, they can be pale pink or salmon colored. Wines labeled "Rosé" are produced in one of two ways. The first is by blending white wine with a small percentage of red wine; the second is by pressing the black-skinned grapes and macerating the juice with the crushed skins just long enough for the juice to take on some color.

There are 357 villages authorized to grow grapes for Champagne production, spread throughout five main areas.

1. **Montagne de Reims** Vineyards are situated south of the city of Reims, where Pinot Noir excels.
2. **Côte des Blancs** Long east-facing slope south and east of the city of Eperney, planted almost exclusively to Chardonnay grapes.
3. **Vallée de la Marne** Stretch of land surrounding the Marne river, encompassing Eperney. Pinot Meunier is the favored grape.
4. **Côte de Sézanne** Small patch of vineyards southwest of the Côte des Blancs.
5. **The Aube** Remote area at the southernmost boundary of the Champagne appellation.

*Gentle effervescence and delicate yet complex flavors make Champagne the unequivocal premium sparkling wine.*

Seventeen villages are deemed the best and are called Grand Cru villages. There are also Premier Cru and Cru designations. Winemakers who use fruit only from Grand Cru or premium Cru villages may use these terms on the wine label. If you're looking for the very best in Champagne, seek out wines from Grand Cru villages. Although the price can often be steep, in most cases the wines are worth it.

The overwhelming success of Champagne prompted producers in other countries to label their sparkling wines "Champagne." Recently though, new rules give protection

*A bottle of sparkling wine with sediment just before the disgorgement process.*

to true Champagne producers. Most of the leading wine countries prohibit their producers from labeling their sparkling wines Champagne. Not all countries have agreed to the terms, so from time to time you may find some wines labeled "Champagne" that hail from outside France. In the United States, producers are banned from using the term unless the label was in use before 2006.

Remember that most premium sparkling wines are produced by a second fermentation that occurs within each bottle. After the base wines are blended, a small amount of *liqueur de tirage* (wine, sugar, and yeast) is added to each bottle and fermentation begins. As the yeast cells die, they form sediment inside the bottle. The extended aging period with the sediment creates Champagne's trademark characteristics: aromas and flavors of toast, brioche, bread, cream, acacia, herbs, and fruit. When the sediment is removed, a process called disgorgement, the wine left behind is clear and pristine. Just before the cork is placed into the bottle, a mixture of liquid sugar and wine, known as the *dosage* or the *liqueur d'expédition*, is added for a final level of sweetness.

*Weather conditions drastically change the amount of Champagne produced each year. As a result, the annual production fluctuates between 250 million to 350 million bottles. On average, Champagne accounts for 10 percent of all the world's sparkling wines.*

---

*For less expensive French sparkling wines, try the following:*

- *Crémant d'Alsace – produced in Alsace, mostly from Pinot Blanc, Pinot Gris, Riesling, and Pinot Noir*
- *Crémant d'Bourgogne – produced in Burgundy, mostly from Aligoté, Chardonnay, Pinot Blanc, and Riesling*
- *Crémant de Jura – produced in Jura, mostly from Chardonnay, Pinot Gris, Pinot Noir, Poulsard, and Savagnin*
- *Crémant de Limoux – produced in the Languedoc-Roussillon, mostly from Mauzac, Chardonnay, and Chenin Blanc*
- *Crémant de Loire – produced in the Loire Valley, mostly from Chenin Blanc*

# From Dry to Sweet

The following categories of Champagne are based on levels of sweetness:

**Brut Nature/Brut Zero**
Bone dry with no added sugar

**Extra Brut**
Nearly bone dry: 0 to 5 grams residual sugar per liter

**Brut**
Very dry: 5 to 15 grams residual sugar per liter

**Extra Sec/Extra Dry**
Off-dry: 2 to 20 grams residual sugar per liter

**Sec/Dry**
Off-dry to lightly sweet: 17 to 35 grams residual sugar per liter

**Demi-Sec**
Medium sweet: 35 to 50 grams residual sugar per liter

**Sec**
Very sweet: more than 50 grams residual sugar per liter

## Buying Champagne

When buying champagne, it is helpful to know the different styles and how they're labeled.

**Non-vintage (NV)** Representing about 80 percent of all the Champagne produced each year, these are made by using base wines from various years to achieve a consistent house style. By law, non-vintage wines must be aged for at least fifteen months before disgorgement of the sediment. While these wines are intended for immediate consumption, they won't spoil if you don't get around to them for a few years.

**Vintage** Vintage-labeled wines are made in the years the grapes are of superior quality. On average, each house produces vintage-labeled wines three years in each decade. By law, all vintage-labeled wines must be aged for at least three years before disgorgment. This extended contact with the lees creates rich and complex wines.

Most collectable wines are aged longer than the minimum. You can age sparkling wines a bit after purchase; however, most should be enjoyed within five to ten years for maximum enjoyment.

**Prestige Cuvée (*Tête de Cuvée*)** These wines are the top bottlings from each house. They're usually produced in vintage years and are made using fruit from the best vineyards and villages. Many of the Prestige Cuvée wines are Blanc de Blanc, Blanc de Noir, or Rosé. This class of Champagne can age for decades after purchase. Over time, they develop dark yellow colors and complex aromas of flint, smoke, and bread, backed by ethereal silky textures. Some of the more popular and collectable wines in this category are:

- "Cuvée Sir Winston Churchill" – Pol Roger
- "Comtes de Champagne" – Taittinger
- "Cristal" – Louis Roederer
- "Grande Siècle" – Laurent-Perrier
- "Dom Pérignon" – Moët et Chandon

The Champagne market is largely driven by firms, or houses, that produce wines using grapes purchased from other farmers. By sourcing many grapes from throughout the region, the winemakers for these larger houses have plenty of options to ensure a consistent house style from year to year. In addition, the larger houses usually own their own vineyards, much of is used to produce the vintage and prestige cuvée wines. In total, Champagne houses market more than half of all Champagne wines, yet own only about 10 percent of the vineyards. They're denoted on wine labels by the letters "NM," meaning *Négociant-Manipulant*.

A big change in Champagne is the growing number of smaller estates that once sold fruit to larger houses and are now producing their own wines. This category of "grower-champagnes" is gaining momentum in the wine world, and enthusiasts are seeking out wines from producers such as Egly-Ouriet, Pierre Gimonnet, Gaston Chiquet, and Jacques Selosse. These grower-producers can offer a more individual product, but the wines are more variable each year due to the discrepancies of each growing season. In some cases they're less expensive than the products from larger houses, but not always. While there are a few thousand grower-champagnes in France, less than 200 are imported to the United States, but this number has been rising, and should continue to rise, in the coming years. You can identify a grower-champagne by the initials "RM" on the label, meaning *Récoltant-Manipulant*.

# Italy

## *Veneto*

Italy's most popular sparkling wine is made from the Prosecco grape, most of which comes from the Veneto in northeastern Italy. Prosecco has long been a fan favorite as a fun, fruity, easygoing sparkling wine. Prosecco sparkling wines are made similar to Champagne, except for one crucial aspect—the secondary fermentation that creates the carbon dioxide is done in large tanks rather than inside individual bottles. When done in this style, the process is called the Charmat Method, or the Tank Method. The finished wine is then bottled afterwards.

The wines' more economical production method results in a fruitier profile with flavors of peaches, pears, and elderflower. They're excellent for drinking on their own or enjoying with food. Prosecco has many culinary uses as well, such as a peppery and zippy *mignonette* sauce for oysters. A staple behind the bar, Prosecco is used for a variety of cocktails, such as the famous Bellini.

While Prosecco is made throughout the region, two towns are noted for their exceptional vineyards and wines— Conegliano and Valdobbiadene, both located about 30 miles (48 km) northwest of Venice. Wines labeled Prosecco di Conegliano, Prosecco di Valdobbiadene, or Prosecco di Conegliano-Valdobbiadene are always made from this part of the Veneto.

Within Valdobbiadene is a sub-zone called Cartizze, where some of the best and most expensive Prosecco is made. Some producers here make wines in the Champagne method, referred to in Italy as the *Metodo Classico*. The wines have a creamier, richer mouthfeel resulting from exposure to the sediment from the dead yeast cells. A variety of refreshing and approachable rosé *(rosato)* sparkling wines is made by blending Prosecco with a little bit of Pinot Noir or other black varieties. Most Prosecco wines are non-vintage.

*Starting in the 1860s, the Carpenè Malvolti estate is credited with revolutionizing the Charmat method and vastly improving the quality of Prosecco.*

*In 2009 the name of the Prosecco grape was changed to Glera. The two names are now used interchangeably on wine labels. Producers are urged to use Glera when referring to the grape and Prosecco when referring to the appellation.*

When purchasing Franciacorta,
it helps to understand the terminology.
Most wines are non-vintage and
labeled Brut. However, there are
a few other distinctions.

**Saten:** *Made only using white grapes, in
this case Chardonnay and Pinot Bianco,
the wines have a slightly lower bottle
pressure than other wines. This results in
a fine and creamy carbonation.*

**Millesimato:** *The Italian term
for vintage.*

**Pas Operé or Pas Dose:** *Used to denote
wines that have received no dosage. In
essence, they're the equivalent to Brut
Nature or Extra Brut Champagne
classifications.*

**Rosé:** *Must be produced from a
minimum of 25 percent Pinot Noir.*

---

*Plenty of Italian producers throughout
Italy make sparkling wines that are
outside the zones of the main four areas.
Some of my favorites are:*

- *Bruno DeConcilis – Fiano/
  Aglianico "Selim" (Campania)*
- *Murgo – Nerello Mascalese Rosé
  (Sicily)*
- *Erpacrife – Nebbiolo (Piemonte)*
- *Colluta – Ribolla Gialla (Friuli)*
- *Bisson – Bianchetta/Vermentino
  "Abissi" (Liguria)*
- *Conti di Buscareto – Lacrima
  (Le Marche)*

## Lombardia

About 150 million bottles of Prosecco are produced each year, dwarfing the output from Italy's other main zone for sparkling wine production: Franciacorta. East of Milan, this zone is Italy's hub for premium sparkling wines, where the rules state that all wines must be made in the Metodo Classico. Annual production hovers around 15 million bottles, most of which come from small properties and producers.

The soil and climate are similar to Champagne's: chalky, limestone-rich soil, and cool temperatures. The stony soil also retains solar energy that aids the vines during the cooler alpine evenings. Neighboring Lake Iseo moderates the temperature in the vineyards by cooling the surrounding air in the summertime and warming the air during the cool autumn months. Since the wines are made like Champagne, they exhibit an elegance and structure that only comes from bottle fermentation. The main grapes used are Chardonnay, Pinot Noir, and Pinot Blanc. As in Champagne, Franciacorta producers craft a variety of wines, including non-vintage, vintage, and premium-vintage wines.

Although sparkling wines have been produced in Lombardia for generations, only since the 1960s have certain wines brought acclaim to the region and inspired other winemakers to attempt the same kind of finished

*Vineyards in Franciacorta at sunset.*

products. Bellavista is the benchmark estate for quality bubbly wines. Started in 1977 by Vittorio Moretti, the estate has excelled in all areas of wine production. Along with native Lombardian winemaker Mattia Vezzola, who joined the winery in 1981, Bellavista has released some impeccable sparkling wines in the past twenty years, helping to draw more attention to northern Italy.

More than a hundred wineries in Franciacorta collectively produce upwards of fifteen million bottles per year. By contrast, some Champagne houses in France single-handedly produce more than fifteen million bottles of wine each year.

*Vineyards of Cantine Ferrari in Trento.*

## Piedmont

In the Piedmont, sparkling wine production is based in the Alta Langa apellation. "Alta" refers to the high elevation vineyards within the Langhe hills, Piedmont's most important wine zone. Chardonnay and Pinot Noir grow well in this climate and are the principle grapes required by law. All Alta Langa sparkling wines must be produced in the classical method.

## Trentino

Quality bubbly is also made in Trento, located in Trentino, Italy's northern region. The climate is cool and the vines grow in a mix of silt and gravel loaded with limestone, remnants of glaciers that retreated from the hills thousands of years ago. The warming effect of the Adige River helps moderate the temperatures for Chardonnay and Pinot Noir throughout the year. Founded in 1902, Cantine Ferrari is the dominant producer and has single-handedly put the region's sparkling wines on the map. Made in the classical method, the wines are fresh, clean, and full of biscuity and toasty aromas. Try their flagship wine, Brut NV, for your everyday sparkling wines and save their top bottle, Giulio Ferrari Riserva del Fondatore, for special occasions.

# Spain

Based in Cataluña, Spain's sparking wine industry dates to the 1870s. In Penedés, producers such as Jose Raventós of Codorníu strove for replicating Champagne-style wines, using the same grapes—Chardonnay and Pinot Noir. The climate wasn't conducive to these grapes, and eventually the producers discovered their own indigenous grapes were much better suited. For many years, producers labeled their wines Champaña, Spanish for "Champagne." After heavy lobbying from Champagne producers, the name for Spain's premier sparkling wine was changed to Cava, Catalan for "cellar." The boundaries for Cava production are rather loose, making it difficult to navigate the different producers, but more than 95 percent of all Cava is produced in Cataluña, and all wines must be produced using the Champagne method.

The three main grapes used for Cava production are Macabeo (Viura), Xarel-lo, and Parellada. The best wines produced from the indigenous grapes are slightly earthy and citrus-based with notes of orange, fennel, and apples. Chardonnay, also used in the blend, has been growing in popularity. It is commonly used in wines that are aged longer before release and contributes body and elegance to the final wine. Rosé (Rosado) Cavas are produced mostly from Garnacha, Monastrell, and Pinot Noir.

*There are three age classifications for Spanish Cava.*

1. *Baseline – 9 months*
2. *Reserva – 15 months*
3. *Gran Reserva – 30 months*

---

*You can spot a bottle of Cava in a wine shop by the four-pointed star marking imprinted on the cork.*

---

*Cava producer Freixenet is the world's largest producer of sparkling wines.*

---

*Cava is the only appellation in Spain that isn't confined to one contiguous geographic area. In 1986, when the EU Wine Authorities announced that appellations must declare specific geographical qualifications as well as rules regarding grapes and production methods, Spanish authorities declared 160 different villages across northern Spain as Cava appellations, mostly encompassing vineyards where grapes were already grown and produced into Cava.*

# New World Sparkling Wines

## United States

The United States wine industry is young by many standards, and collectively we're still learning more about our tastes as consumers and more about which grapes to grow in which regions. As a result, there's yet to be a defined area specifically devoted to sparkling wines. In the coming years, producers in California and also in New York and New Mexico will begin to establish themselves as the torchbearers for American bubbly. Since the majority of American wine comes from California, it is no surprise there are plenty to try from the Golden State. Most are produced in the cooler regions of California, such as Carneros, Anderson Valley, the Russian River

*In 1892 the Korbel Brothers, Bohemian immigrants, produced the first American sparkling wine.*

---

*Recommended California Sparkling Wine Producers:*

- *Domaine Carneros – Carneros*
- *Domaine Chandon – Napa Valley*
- *Gloria Ferrer – Carnernos*
- *Handley Cellars – Anderson Valley*
- *Iron Horse – Green Valley*
- *J – Russian River Valley*
- *Roederer Estate – Anderson Valley*
- *Scharffenberger – Mendocino County*
- *Schramsberg – North Coast*
- *Sea Smoke – Santa Rita Hills*
- *Piper Sonoma – Sonoma*
- *Riverbench – Santa Maria Valley*
- *V. Sattui – Napa Valley*

Valley, Santa Maria Valley, and the Santa Rita Hills. Many of the best sparkling wines are made in the Champagne method from Chardonnay and Pinot Noir and aim to emulate the style (and success) of Champagne, France.

The Finger Lakes appellation in New York has proven to be a great region for sparkling wines, many of which are produced from Riesling and other white grapes. Look for New York sparkling wines from Damiani Wine Company, Douglas Hill Winery, Fox Run Vineyards, Glenora Wine Cellars, Goose Watch Winery, Red Tail Ridge, and America's longest-continually operating winery, Brotherhood Winery.

New Mexico was once a thriving wine state, with records of vineyards dating to the 1629 when monks planted the Mission grape. By the late 1880s it was the fifth leading state in wine production. Following Prohibition, winemakers were late to arrive in New Mexico but were happy to find that the warm hot days and cool nights were perfect for wine production. There are now more than forty wineries in the state. Many of the best vineyards are within the Rio Grande River Valley, led by the Gruet Winery. It was founded in 1987 by Luarent Gruet and Farid Himeur, formerly of Champagne, France.

## Other Sparkling Wines

When seeking out a new sparkling wine, check the label for information about which grapes are used, how the wine is made (Champagne method versus Charmat method), and where it comes from. If there's one thing that wine enthusiasts can agree on, it's that quality sparkling wines should come from cooler climates. Germany and Austria produce excellent sparkling wines, mostly from Riesling and Grüner Veltliner, respectively. Australia, Argentina, Canada, and England are also good bets for bubbly.

# Dessert Wines

The majority of the world's greatest dessert wines are made by using overly ripe and/or dried grapes and then arresting alcoholic fermentation to retain some of the grape's natural sugars. Although most dessert wines are made using white varieties, some fantastic dessert wines are made from red grapes as well. Regardless of color, the secret to making a great dessert wine is finding the right balance between sugar and acidity. If there's too much sugar, the wines will taste syrupy and sticky and lack structure and balance. Growers are adamant about using only the best grapes at the right time, so they often pick the grapes in tries, going through the vineyard several times over the course of a few weeks. Vineyard workers walk up and down the rows of vineyards and handpick only the grapes that are ripe enough. A day or so later, they retrace their steps and cut away a few more bunches, leaving behind those that still need to mature. They repeat these steps until most, if not all, grapes are harvested. If they wait too long, however, a sudden frost can arise and the remaining grapes will be lost.

## France

The most famous dessert wines in the world hail from Sauternes, Barsac, and Bergerac, appellations in Bordeaux and southwestern France. Based on Sauvignon Blanc and Sémillon grapes, the wines have silky textures with intoxicating flavors of dried apricots, peaches, pineapple, and spices such as clove and anise. The blend of the two grapes is a perfect union as the zippy and crisp character of Sauvignon Blanc blends well with the unctuous and rich body of Sémillon. A third grape, Muscadelle, is also used, but usually in small doses. Age-worthy and regal, the wines develop deep golden colors and complex aromas of dried fruits and spices.

In the Loire Valley, the Chenin Blanc grape makes complex dessert wines, most notably in the appellations of Savennières, Coteaux du Layon, and Bonnezeaux. Further east in France, the dry conditions in Alsace give winemakers the luxury of leaving their grapes on the vine well into the autumn months. Wines produced from late-harvested grapes infected with *botrytis cinerea* are labeled *Sélection de Grains Nobles*. The preferred grapes are Riesling, Pinot Gris, Gewürztraminer, and Muscat.

*Winemakers are exhilarated when* botrytis cinerea *makes an appearance in the vineyard. A fungus that feeds on the moisture within grapes,* botrytis cinerea *needs prolonged warm and humid conditions to flourish. As the fungus attacks the skins, it draws water from the grapes by as much as two-thirds, thereby concentrating sugars and acidity. The overwhelming majority of age-worthy and collectable dessert wines are made from grapes infected with* botrytis cinerea, *also known as "noble rot."*

*Opposite page: Tannat grapes drying on the vine well into the autumn months in Uruguay.*

*Moscato – the grape of choice in Piedmont, Italy, where it's used to make a wide variety of dessert wines.*

# Italy

The Piedmont region is home to some of the country's most important dessert wines. Moscato d'Asti and Asti Spumante are both produced from Moscato in the province of Asti. They range from slightly fizzy, or *frizzante*, to fully sparkling. Best enjoyed in their youth, the wines' signature flavors of peaches, pears, and elderflower wane over time. Although lesser known, Brachetto d'Acqui is a *frizzante* red wine with sweet flavors of black cherries and cranberries produced in the province of Acqui.

In the Veneto region, winemakers use dried grapes to produce highly concentrated red dessert wines labeled *Recioto della Valpolicella*. Corvina grapes are dried at the winery in elaborate huts with drying racks and fans. Other times the grape bunches are hung from overhead rafters to slowly dry before pressing. This method of drying grapes to concentrate their sugars is called *appassimento*. The wines are rich with flavors of dark black cherries, leather, prunes, and baking spices.

Tuscany is known for Vin Santo ("Wine of the Saints"), a wine made from dried Trebbiano and Malvasia grapes. The grapes are traditionally dried until the week before Easter and then crushed to make juice. The wine ferments very slowly for a few years in 50-liter (13-gallon) barrels before bottling. The finished wines are dark amber in color with sweet, citrusy notes and almond and nutty flavors.

Sicily has two unique island appellations for dessert wine. In the northeast, on the islands of Lipari and Solinas, producers use Malvasia grapes to make light and quaffy Malvasia delle Lipari dessert wines. In the southwest, on the island of Pantelleria between Sicily and Tunisia, Moscato is grown to make darker and more robust dessert wines. The grape is locally referred to as Zibibbo, and the wines are called Passito di Pantelleria.

*Dried Corvina grapes at the Allegrini winery before pressing to make recioto and amarone wine.*

# Hungary

Hungary's most significant contribution to the world of wine is its sweet dessert wine made in the Tokaj region, one of Europe's earliest classified zones dating to the 1700s. Ever since, Tokaj's sweet wines have been favored by the kings and queens of Europe. Based on Furmint, an indigenous grape, the wines are amber in color and intoxicatingly complex, created by years of cask aging. "Tokaji Esszencia" wines are made using the free-run juice from grape bunches placed into large capacity containers. The weight of the grape bunches on top gently crush the grapes on the bottom, creating a miniscule amount of clear juice that's considered superior to juice obtained from traditionally pressed grapes.

## Ice Wine

Germany, Austria, and Canada are known for their sweet dessert wines produced from frozen grapes. Whether made from white grapes such as Riesling, Grüner Veltliner, or Vidal Blanc, or from red grapes such as Cabernet Franc, the grapes are picked after they have frozen on the vines. Winemakers patiently wait for the first frost and then must act quickly to harvest the grapes. Crushed before they defrost, the water inside the grape stays frozen, consequently concentrating the sugar and acidity. Due to the limited supply of frozen grapes, ice wine is rare and expensive wherever it is produced.

*Vineyards on the shores of Lake Balaton in Hungary.*

# Fortified Wines

Fortified wines are made by adding a neutral spirit either during or after fermentation. Adding alcohol is one way to control fermentation. Most yeast cells can only transfer sugar into alcohol below 17 percent. Once the alcohol reaches this level, the yeast cells are inactive. Fortification, the addition of alcohol, does the job by increasing the percentage of alcohol.

Fortified wine production is centered in Europe. Portugal is famous for its port wine, produced in the northern region of the country, and also for Madeira, produced on an island southwest of the country. Spain's contribution to fortified wines is sherry, produced in Andalucía in the southwestern corner of the country. Most sherry is dry to off-dry, but some sweet sherry is also produced. Marsala is Italy's most important fortified wine, produced on the western side of Sicily.

## Port

Port is produced in the Duoro Valley in northern Portugal, one of the oldest regulated wine zones in the world. Many of the vines grow on the steep, terraced vineyards throughout the valley. The main grapes for red port are Touriga Nacional, Touriga Francesca, Tinta Roriz, Tina Cão, Tinta Barroca, Tinta Amarela, Tinta Francisca, Bastardo, and Mourisco. These grapes must constitute a minimum of 60 percent of the blend. Produced in lower quantities, white port is made from Gouveio, Malvasia Fina, Viosinho, Rabigato, Esgana Cão, and Folgasão.

Port is made by adding alcohol to fermenting juice. Following the harvest, grapes are brought to the winery and crushed. The skins (and stems if they're left) remain with the juice. Fermentation begins while the skins and juice are macerating. After a few days, the partially fermented wine is separated from the solids and grape skins. This usually occurs when about one third of the sugar has been converted into alcohol. Alcohol is then added to fortify the wine to about 20 percent.

While not all fortified wines are sweet, most fall under the category of "dessert wines."

---

Vermouth and other wine-based cordials are fortified wines that have been flavored with herbs, spices, and roots. This group is categorized as "aromatized wines."

---

The port market is similar to Champagne's. Large port houses purchase fruit from a network of farmers. Each year, reserves are stored so that the winemaker can blend different years together to consistently produce the same style.

---

Only vintage port is worthy of being aged; all other port wines are ready to drink when purchased.

---

Adding alcohol to wine is known as "beneficio" in Portuguese. "Aguardente" roughly translates to "burning water" and is the 77 percent alcohol grape spirit that is added to fermenting port wine.

Most port is sold as either ruby or tawny. Ruby port is aged in barrels or tanks for a few years prior to bottling. When conditions are right and the grapes are exceptional, a vintage ruby port will be produced. Vintage-labeled ruby port is the most age-worthy expression of port, and also the most expensive. Only 1 to 3 percent of all the port made each year carries a vintage. These wines must be decanted as the bottles develop heavy loads of sediment over decades. Overall, ruby port is deeply colored and fruit-driven.

Tawny port is lighter in color, a result of less extraction of color from the skins, and sometimes from the blending with white port. Most tawny port has an indication of its age, such as "10 year," "20 year," "30 year," or "40 year" tawny. As tawny port ages in casks, the wines dissipate in color and take on brown and amber colors. "20 Year Tawny" is very popular because the wines have a balance of fruit and mature characteristics, without the extreme nuttiness and oxidative qualities that some older tawny port can bring.

*Port aging in large casks and barrels at Taylor Fladgate.*

## Madeira

Madeira is a fortified wine from the islands of Madeira and Porto Santo, islands southwest of Portugal's mainland. Originally, dry table wines were shipped from Madeira in wood barrels. As they were transported through the tropics, the wines were exposed to high temperatures. Upon arriving to their destination, the wines were transformed into brown wines with nutty and caramel flavors. This style of wine came to be known as "madeirized."

Today, modern methods basically "pre-cook" the wines before bottling. Using heat and oxidation—two ways to destroy a wine—Madeira producers slowly and methodically produce fragrant and acidic wines. After pressing, fermentation, and fortification, the wines are exposed to heat, either in tanks where internal coils are heated with steam and hot water, or in barrels placed in warm rooms and huts. When in barrels, the slow oxidation, heating, and evaporation give the wines concentrated nutty aromas and tangy, burnt-caramel, and slightly bitter flavors.

The main noble grapes are Sercial, Verdelho, Baol, and Malvasia (Malmsey). Sercial is considered the driest version of Madeira, and Malvasia is known for making sweeter and softer versions. A fifth grape, Tinta Negra, is also used, but is considered inferior to the previous four grapes. Madeira wines that have no grape on the label are most likely made from this outlier. Similar to port, vintage-labeled Madeiras, called Frasqueiras, are the most expensive and age-worthy. Due to the high alcohol content, a bottle of Madeira, like port, can last weeks (if not months) after opening, before losing most of its positive attributes.

*Referring to Madeira, "Estufagem" is the process of heating wine in tanks for a few months, and "Canteiro" is the process of heating barrels of wine for years on end.*

---

*The production of Madeira is overseen by the Embroidery and Handicraft Institute of Madeira (IVBAM), which regulates harvesting and production methods.*

**Opposite page:** *The Valley of the Nuns in Madeira.*

*Three towns compose the sherry triangle. All sherry must be shipped from one of these three:*

1. *Jerez de la Frontera*
2. *El Puerto de Santa Maria*
3. *Sanlúcar de Barrameda*

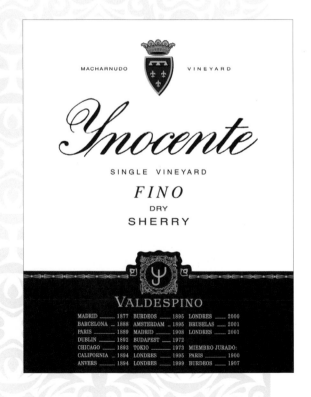

## Sherry

The Moors conquered Spain in 711, and although wine was officially outlawed, wine production probably continued, according to records of wine taxation. The Moors introduced distillation to the Spanish, first for medical purposes and then for brandy. To this end, fortification was applied to wine, and thus was born sherry, Spain's most unique wine.

Sherry is produced in Andalucía in southwestern Spain and the process is part of what makes sherry so unique. The Jerez appellation is Spain's hottest zone, and grapes like Palomino, Pedro Ximénez, and Moscatel grow well in the sandy, clay, and chalk soils. When the grapes are ripe, they're brought to the winery for crushing and fermenting. After fermentation concludes, the best wines are fortified to about 15 percent alcohol and placed into casks. By springtime some of the casks develop a thin film on the top of the wine. This thin film, called *flor*, absorbs trace amounts of residual sugar, lowers acids, and adds creamy and nutty flavors. It also prevents the wines from over oxidation. Casks that fully develop flor are called *fino*, and those where the flor has only partially developed are called *oloroso*. Once classified, they're blended with older sherry wines of the same type in an organized system called *solera*.

The solera system is built on the idea of blending a bit of old wine with a good amount of new wine and replenishing the old barrels with young wine, rather than depleting old barrels altogether. Each year, about one-fourth to one-third of the wine from the oldest barrels is taken for bottling. The wine that was drawn off is replenished with wine from the second oldest tier of wines, which is replaced with a younger wine from the next level, and so on all the way up to the youngest solera. This method allows producers to keep a consistent house-style. Blending new wine with old infuses the youthful character into the old wine, while bestowing the mature characteristics into the new wine. Some solera systems have dozens of wines of varying ages. While best known in Spain, the solera system is used in other countries as well.

## Styles of Sherry

**Amontillado** An aged Fino Sherry. Authentic Amontillado Sherry is always dry.

**Cream Sherry** Oloroso Sherry blended with sweet dessert wine. Cream Sherry is usually offered as a dessert wine.

**Manzanilla** Fino Sherry that comes from the town of Sanlúcar de Barrameda. Some take on subtle saline notes, ideal for fresh seafood tapas.

**Palo Cortado** Oloroso Sherry that was once from barrels with levels of flor that completely covered the wine in the barrel, but eventually receded and turned to oloroso. They showcase the dry character of sherry with more oxidative aromas and flavors.

*The "mar de botas" or sea of barrels at Valdespino.*

## Marsala

Marsala is a fortified wine produced mostly from the indigenous grapes Grillo and Catarratto. While once ranked in the same company as port, sherry, and Madeira, today over-production has reduced it to a liquid used for cooking veal or chicken. At its best, Marsala is a complex wine with strong nutty profiles and balanced flavors of golden raisins and honey. A few producers in Sicily still focus on Marsala and put out world-class fortified wines that can go head-to-head with the best from Portugal and Spain. Look for Marsala from Marco de Bartoli for the very best from Sicily.

Depending on the type of grapes used, Marsala is divided into three classifications: *oro*, *ambra*, and *rubino*. *Oro* (gold) and *ambra* (amber) are produced from white grapes. *Rubino* (ruby) is produced from black grapes. There is a secondary classification system based on age. *Fine* Marsala, aged for about one year, is predominantly used for cooking. *Superiore* Marsala is aged a minimum of two years and *Superiore Riserva* Marsala is aged for four years. Marsala can be either sweet or dry, and producers label the wines as such: *secco* (dry) and *dolce* (sweet).

*Sherry aging at Valdespino in Andalucia.*

Marsala labeled *Vergine* or *Soleras* is the most intense and complex of all. Aged for a minimum of five years, the wines are dry with aromas of nuts, orange peel, and spice. Known for its oxidative nutty and savory sweet qualities, these types of Marsala are an excellent companion to a wide range of desserts.

# Resources

Throughout my career, I've been asked for recommendations on books, readings, and web sites that are helpful for the beginner wine drinker. Below are some of the resources that have helped shape the foundation of my wine education.

## General Reference

Bastianich, Joseph and David Lynch. *The Regional Wines of Italy*. New York: Clarkson Potter, 2005.

Clarke, Oz. *Oz Clarke's New Encyclopedia of Wine: The Complete World of Wine, From Abruzzo to Zinfandel*. London: Webster's International Publishers Limited, 2003.

Herbst, Ron and Sharon Tyler Herbst. *The New Wine Lover's Companion: Second Edition*. New York: Barron's Educational Series, 2003.

Poyet, Elizabeth. *The Little Black Book of Wine: A Simple Guide to the World of Wine*. White Plains: Peter Pauper Press, 2004.

Robinson, Andrea. *Great Wine Made Simple: Straight Talk from a Master Sommelier*. New York: Clarkson Potter, 2005.

Robinson, Jancis. *How to Taste: A Guide to Enjoying Wine*. New York: Simon & Schuster, 2008.

Robinson, Jancis, editor. *The Oxford Companion to Wine*. Oxford: Oxford University Press, 1999.

Stevenson, Tom. *The Sotheby's Wine Encyclopedia: The Classic Reference to the Wines of the World, 4th Edition*. New York: Dorling Kindersley Publishers, 2005.

Zraly, Kevin. *Windows on the World: Complete Wine Course, 2006 Edition*. New York: Sterling Publishing Co., Inc., 2005.

## Pairing Food and Wine

Dornenburg, Andrew and Karen Page. *What to Drink with What You Eat: The Definitive Guide to Pairing Food with Wine, Beer, Spirits, Coffee, Tea—Even Water—Based on Expert Advice from America's Best Sommeliers*. New York: Bulfinch Press, 2006.

Goldstein, Evan. *Perfect Pairings: A Master Sommelier's Practical Advice for Partnering Wine with Food*. Berkeley and Los Angeles: University of California Press, 2006.

## Also of Interest

Bastianich, Joseph. *Grandi Vini: An Opinionated Tour of Italy's 89 Finest Wines*. New York: Clarkson Potter, 2010.

McInerney, Jay. *The Juice: Vinous Veritas*. New York: Alfred A. Knopf, 2012.

Pinney, Thomas. *The Makers of American Wine: A Record of Two Hundred Years*. Berkeley, California: University of California Press, 2012.

Taber, George M. *Judgment of Paris: California vs. France and the Historic 1976 Paris Tasting That Revolutionized Wine*. New York: Scribner, 2005.

Taber, George M. *To Cork or Not To Cork: Tradition, Romance, Science, and the Battle for the Wine Bottle*. New York: Scribner, 2007.

Theise, Terry. *Reading Between the Vines*. Berkeley, California: University of California Press, 2010.

Wallace, Benjamin. *The Billionaire's Vinegar: The Mystery of the World's Most Expensive Bottle of Wine*. New York: Three Rivers Press, 2008.

## Web Sites and Blogs

**www.thewinedoctor.com**
Wine expert Chris Kissack's *The Wine Doctor* blog covers a wide range of wine topics.

**wineeconomist.com**
*The Wine Economist* is author Mike Veseth's blog, which analyzes and interprets today's global wine markets.

**www.wineforthestudent.com**
*Wine for the Student* is author Dan Amatuzzi's web site about all things wine.

# Glossary

**Acid** – a taste component of wine that gives wine its lively and fresh character.

**Acidic** – a term used to describe high levels of acid in wines, usually wines that are tart and sharp.

**Aerating** – the action of exposing wine to oxygen in order to release the aromas and flavors.

**American Viticultural Area (AVA)** – a classified growing area set forth and delineated by the U.S. government.

**Appellation** – a delimited zone that specifies certain rules and regulations which all winemakers in that appellation must follow. Every major wine-producing country has an appellation system that helps to classify and differentiate its wines.

**Appellation d'Origine Contrôlée (AOC)** – the French system of appellations that delimits geography, grape varieties, aging requirements, and other criteria.

**Aroma** – the smell and fragrance of a wine.

**Austere** – a term used to describe wine with astringent tannins and high in acid yet lacking body and roundness.

**Balance** – a positive term used to express the equal proportions of certain characteristics of wine, usually referring to alcohol, tannin, acidity, fruitiness, and bitterness.

**Barrique** –a wood barrel that holds about 225 liters (60 gallons). It is the most popular size used throughout the world to mature wine.

**Bâtonnage** – a winemaking term for stirring of the lees during the aging and maturation of a wine. It reinvigorates the yeast cells back into the wine and results in extra round and creamy textures.

**Bead** – a term used to describe the stream of tiny bubbles in a sparkling wine.

**Big** – a term used to describe a wine that has lots of power, color, fruit, and/or alcohol.

**Blending** – a winemaking practice that involves using numerous wines to make a desired finished product.

**Body** – a term used to describe the color and texture of wine. The three terms most often used are light-bodied, medium-bodied, and full-bodied.

**Botrytis cinerea (bo-TRY-tis sin-AIR-ee-a)** – a beneficial mold that occurs in very specific conditions and is a contributing factor to making elite dessert wines. Also called "noble rot."

**Bouquet** – the collection of aromas and scents that a wine emits.

**Breathe** – to expose wine to air so that it is more approachable. In the absence of oxygen, wines can be muted and closed.

**Brut (broot)** – French term used on wine labels to describe a dry sparkling wine.

**Canopy** – the collection and strategic position of leaves to shield and protect grapes from sun, wind, and other elements.

**Champagne method** – a method of sparkling wine production where the secondary fermentation is done in individual bottles. Afterwards, the sediment is expelled and a final dosage, an additional wine or spirit, is added to alter the level of sweetness. Considered the best method for making sparkling wines, the process takes its name from Champagne, France, where the top sparkling wines in the world are produced using this method.

**Charmat method** – a method of sparkling wine production where the secondary fermentation is done in large tanks and the wines are individually bottled afterwards. Also known as the tank method.

**Chewy** – a term used to describe wines with powerful tannins, which leave a gripping and astringent mouthfeel.

**Closed** – a term used to describe young, undeveloped red wines with little aroma and flavor. Breathing can sometimes help open up the wine.

**Cloudy** – a term used to describe a wine's dull and hazy appearance. In some cases, a cloudy wine is a negative quality due to a winemaking flaw; at other times, a cloudy wine is a result of non-filtration.

**Complex** – a positive term used to describe a wine's combination of elegance, richness, alcohol, acidity, balance, and flavor.

**Corked** – a term used for wine affected by cork taint. Corked wines exhibit aromas of damp mold and musty characters.

**Crisp** – a term used to describe wine that is light, sharp, refreshing, and clean.

**Cru (crew)** – French for "growth." Refers to a specific vineyard or collection of vineyards.

**Cuvée (koo-VAY)** – a high-end or superior wine.

**Decanting** – transferring a wine from its bottle to another bottle or container to separate the wine from any sediment and to help the wine breathe.

**Demi-sec** – a classification of sparkling wines that are slightly to medium sweet.

**Disgorgement** – From the French term dégorgement (day-gorzh-MOWN); the process of expelling sediment from a bottle of sparkling wine following secondary fermentation.

**Dosage (doh-SAHZH)** – a mixture of wine and sugar, and sometimes brandy or citric acid that is added to a recently disgorged sparkling wine just after the sediment from secondary fermentation has been expelled. The sweetness level of the dosage will determine the overall level of sweetness in the wine.

**Dry** – a term used to describe wine with no perceptible flavor of sugar or sweetness. If all the sugar in grape juice is fermented into alcohol, then the wine is deemed dry, regardless if the wine tastes fruity or juicy.

**Earthy** – aroma or flavor reminiscent of rich, damp soil. It is usually a positive attribute of wine, but can be a negative if it is too pronounced.

**Elegant** – a positive term for a wine that is refined, balanced, and appealing.

**Extract** – a term used to describe the richness, depth, concentration, and flavor of the fruit qualities in a wine.

**Extra dry** – a misleading term used to describe sparkling wines that are off-dry to slightly sweet.

**Fermentation** – the process of transferring the sugar in grape juice into alcohol.

**Field blend** – a blended wine made by incorporating all the different grape varieties in a vineyard or on a property.

**Fining** – a technique for clarifying a wine by adding ingredients such as bentonite or egg whites, which attract sediment and other particles leftover from fermentation and maceration.

**Finish** – the aftertaste or final sensations that linger in the mouth after the wine is tasted. High-quality wines have long and complex finishes.

**Flabby** – a term used to describe wine that lacks acidity and tastes overly rich and weighty.

**Flat** – a negative term for wine that tastes dull and weak due to a lack of acidity and structure. It is also used to describe a sparkling wine that has lost its carbonation.

**Fleshy** – a term used to describe a wine that has balanced texture, extract, and tannin and induces a sensation like biting into a ripe apple, plum, or other fruit.

**Flinty** – an aroma or flavor descriptor of flint striking rocks or steel. Usually used to describe white wines that originate in certain limestone and gravel-rich soils.

**Flor (floor)** – a thin layer of yeast that sometimes forms on the surface of sherry during fermentation.

**Flute** – a tall and slender wineglass commonly used to serve sparkling wine.

**Fortified wine** – wines with added alcohol.

**Frizzante (free-DZAHN-teh)** – Italian term for a semi-sparkling wine, such as Moscato d'Asti, Brachetto d'Acqui and some types of Lambrusco.

**Fruity** – a term used to describe wines that offer aromas and flavors of fruits such as apples, pears, peaches, plums, and berries.

**Full-bodied** – a term used to describe wine that is rich, opulent, and deep in color and flavor.

**Grand Cru (grawn crew)** – French term for "great growth." It is the highest designation for a single vineyard wine. It is most relevant to vineyards in Burgundy, Alsace, and Champagne where the soil and aspect change rapidly and small, adjacent parcels of land can create very different wines.

**Grassy** – a term used to describe wine that emits aromas of freshly cut grass, typical of Sauvignon Blanc.

**Halbtrocken (HAHLP-trahk-en)** – a German term for half-dry or medium-dry wines.

**Hazy** – a term used to describe wines that are cloudy or not clear due to a lack of fining or filtration.

**Hebaceous** – a term used to describe the aroma of herbs in a wine, such as oregano, rosemary, basil, or mint. It is usually a positive attribute. If the aromas are pungent and strong, the wines are described as being vegetal.

**Hybrid** – a grapevine made by crossing two different species of grapes and creating a completely new grape variety with its own flowering properties and leaf structures.

**Intensity** – refers to the concentration of color in a wine. Softer and lighter wines are said to have a pale intensity, while darker and more opaque-colored wines have a dark intensity.

**Kabinett (kah-bee-NETT)** – a German classification of wine based on the ripeness level and sugar content of the grapes.

**Lactic acid** – an acid created in wine during the malolactic fermentation process. Its presence in wine is noticeable by round and creamy textures.

**Late harvest** – a term used to describe wine made from grapes left on the vine longer than usual.

**Lees** – the dead and expired yeast cells following fermentation.

**Legs** – the streaks that wine leaves behind on the sides of a glass as it is swirled.

**Light-bodied** – a term used to express wine that is light, soft, and easy-going and lacking heavy sensations of fruit, flavor, alcohol, and so on.

**Maceration** – the process of keeping the crushed skins in contact with the fresh grape juice.

**Maderized** – a term used to describe the undesirable nutty and oxidized qualities of a dry table wine, usually occurring from oxidation in the bottle. Maderized is a positive attribute when discussing Madeira, a fortified wine that, when made correctly by intentional cooking and oxidizing, emits intoxicating aromas of caramel, toffee, and nuts.

**Magnum** – the equivalent of two standard bottles of wine, or 1.5 liter (1.5 quarts).

**Malic acid** – a natural acid in grapes, similar to the crisp and sharp acid found in Granny Smith apples.

**Malolactic fermentation** – a bacterial-induced secondary fermentation that transfers the sharp and crisp malic acid into the creamy and rounder lactic acid. No alcohol is produced.

**Mature** – a term used to describe perfectly-aged wines that are neither too young nor too old. It is a positive term when applied to older wines that display balanced aromas and flavors.

**Meaty** – a term for wine that displays aromas and flavors of savory meat, bacon, cowhide, and leather.

**Meritage** – an American term for a blended wine made from Bordeaux grape varieties.

**Mouthfeel** – the feel of a wine's texture and flavor in one's mouth. Elements in a wine that contribute to mouthfeel are acidity, alcohol, tannin, bitterness, and sugar. Common terms to describe mouthfeel are rough, soft, powerful, silky, and smooth.

**Must** – the juice of freshly crushed grapes before it is produced into wine.

**New World** – a term applied to non-European winemaking countries, which, on average, have younger wine cultures than European countries.

**Noble rot** – See *Botrytis cinerea*.

**Noble varieties** – grapes from Europe's main wine zones that are cultivated throughout the world and are the most recognizable among consumers.

**Non-vintage** – wine made from blends of different years, enabling the winemaker to craft a consistent wine year after year. Commonly done with sparkling and fortified wines.

**Nose** – a general term used to describe a wine's aroma.

**Nutty** – a term used for wines that display aromas or flavors of any nut, including almonds, walnuts, peanuts, and so on.

**Oaky** – a term used to describe the aromas and flavors imparted to a wine by oak barrels and casks.

**Off-dry** – a term used to identify and label wines that have the slightest hint of sweetness.

**Old World** – a term applied to European winemaking countries, which on average have older wine cultures than other wine-producing countries.

**Oxidized** – refers to wines that have been exposed to air for a prolonged period of time. The color is usually brownish and smells like nuts and damp fruits. Also called "sherry-like" or "maderized."

**Peak** – the period of time when a wine is best for drinking. Most wines are meant to be consumed young, but wines intended for some aging are less enjoyable in their youth due to gripping and astringent tannins. Each wine's peak is different.

**Peppery** – a term used to describe wine that displays flavors or aromas of spice.

**Phylloxera (fill-LOCK-she-rah)** – a vine aphid or louse that attacks the root system of grapevines.

**Polyphenol** – compounds found in the skins, seeds, and pits of grapes that aid in the prevention of degenerative diseases such as heart disease and cancer.

**Pomace** – the residue of grape skins, seeds, pits, and pulp after the grapes have been crushed and separated from the juice either before or after fermentation. Sometimes pomace is distilled to make grape spirits, such as brandy.

**Pulp** – the juicy inner part of the grape.

**Punt** – the dimple or indentation at the bottom of a wine bottle.

**Qualitätswein mit Pradikat (QmP) (Kval-ee-TEHTS-vine mit PREH-dee-kaht)** – the highest level of distinction for German wines, meaning "quality with distinction."

**Racking** – the process of transferring wine from one barrel or tank to another. This helps clarify the wine since the sediment at the bottom of the tank is left behind as the wine is siphoned off.

**Racy** – a term used to describe wine that is light in body and highly acidic.

**Raisiny** – a term used to describe wine with aromas and flavors of prunes, dates, or other dried fruits.

**Reserve** – a term applied to wine perceived to be of a higher quality than other wines of its type. The rules for reserve wines vary, so there is no guarantee that a reserve wine is more exceptional.

**Residual sugar (RS)** – any grape sugar that was not transferred into alcohol during fermentation and remains preserved in the wine. Many dry table wines have indiscernible traces of residual sugar. Other wines are intentionally made by arresting fermentation and keeping certain sugars to add body and sweetness to the wine.

**Riddling** – the process of slowly rotating and inverting bottles of sparkling wine as they age in order to shift sediment toward the cork.

**Ripe** – a term used to describe wine that has the flavor and aroma of juicy, ripe fruits.

**Robust** – a term used to describe wine that is round, big, and powerful.

**Round** – a term used to describe wine that has a smooth and well-balanced velvety texture.

**Rough** – a term used to describe wine that is tannic and coarse.

**Sec** – a French term used to describe a dry wine. When used to describe sparkling wines, however, it means sweet.

**Secondary fermentation** – the process of conducting a second alcoholic fermentation to produce sparkling wine by trapping carbon dioxide that is produced.

**Sediment** – the particles left after fermentation. Also the solid residue that forms in bottles of red wines as the wine matures.

**Smoky** – a term used to describe wine that has a smoky flavor and aroma, usually due to the soil where the grapes were grown or to any oak barrels that were used in the process of making the wine.

**Sommelier (so-mel-YAY)** – the server or manager in a restaurant who specializes in wine service.

**Sparkling wine** – wine produced by trapping the carbon dioxide resulting from alcoholic fermentation.

**Spicy** – a term used to describe wine with spicy and peppery notes.

**Spumante** – Italian for "sparkling" and referring to sparkling wine.

**Stemmy** - a term that describes wine with bitter, vegetal, and astringent flavors and textures, usually resulting from extended contact with the stems and skins during maceration. Also called "stalky."

**Sulfites** – the salts of sulfurous acids, which preserve wine by preventing spoilage. Created in small amounts during fermentation, sulfites are usually added to wine to arrest fermentation and stabilize the wine.

**Supple** – a term used to describe wines that are well balanced with pleasing qualities such as ripe fruit flavors and gentle, velvety tannins.

**Sur lie (soor LEE)** – French for "on the lees," the term refers to the process of aging wines with the spent yeast cells that form during fermentation.

**Table wine** – a general term for any still wine ranging between 7 and 14 percent alcohol.

**Tank method** – see Charmat method.

**Tannin** – a substance found in the skins, stems, and pits of grapes. When the juice macerates with the skins prior to or during fermentation, the

tannin leeches into the finished wine. Tannin is characterized by astringent and chewy sensations felt between the cheek and the gums.

**Terroir (teh-RWAHR)** – French for "soil," the term refers to all the elements that make up a vineyard's growing conditions, such as soil, slope, drainage, altitude, and climate.

**Thin** – a term used to describe wine lacking in body and structure.

**Toasty** – a term used to describe wine with the aroma and flavors of crispy toast and breadcrumbs. It is the result of oak barrel maturation, especially when the staves of the barrel were significantly charred before the barrel was constructed.

**Trellising** – a method of training leaves onto wire or other support systems that promotes new shoots, exposes grape bunches to solar rays, and helps aerate grapes and fend off rot.

**Trocken** – German for "dry," meaning little to no residual sugar is in the wine.

**Vanilla** – refers to a wine that displays aromas and flavors of vanilla and cream, resulting from oak barrel maturation, typically French oak barrels.

**Varietal** – a wine made from just one type of grape, sometimes called a "mono-varietal" wine.

**Variety** – a type of grape within one grape species.

**Vegetal** – a term used to describe a wine with green and earthy aromas and flavors.

**Velvety** – a term used to describe wine that is smooth and silky and low in acid and tannin.

**Vintage** – the year in which the grapes were grown and produced into wine.

**Viticulture** – the science of the cultivation of grapes.

**Vitis vinifera (VEE-tiss vih-NIFF-er-ah)** – the dominant grapevine species that produces grapes to make wine.

**Yeast** – living, microscopic, single-cell organisms responsible for turning grape juice into wine.

**Yield** – a measure of the quantity of wine produced.

# ACKNOWLEDGEMENTS

I'd like to thank Lourdes, Mom and Dad, my brothers Nick and Chris, Michael Hill Smith, Joe Bastianich, Mario Batali, Lidia Bastianich, Diego Avanzato, Dan Drohan, Ryan Buttner, Evan Goldstein, Valter Scarbolo, Valter and Nadia Fissore, Nick Radisic, Alex and Adam Saper, Alex Pilas, Tracey Bachman, Mark Ladner, the Farinetti family, Jamie Stewart, Federico Zanuso, Marcello Lunelli and the rest of the Ferrari family, Patricia Toth, David Lynch, Penny Murray and the rest of the Planeta family, all the sommeliers who have helped me along the way, and every great winemaker for producing the stuff that dreams are made of.

# PHOTO CREDITS

# INDEX

decanting, 80–81
dessert wines, 14, 43, 60, 204–207. *See also* fortified wines
disgorgement, 193
distribution, 54, 98–99, 132
Domaine Carneros, 173, 202
Dominus Estate, 173
Doux (sweet), 106
Dr. Konstantin Frank, 142
dry wines, 124, 194
Dufour, John James, 128
dumping, 94

E. & J. Gallo Winery, 104, 131
18th Amendment (Prohibition), 128, 131
elevation, 36, 116, 126, 144
Embroidery and Handicraft Institute of Madeira (IVBAM), 211
England, 126–127
environment, 46–47, 145, 148, 177
estate-bottled wines, 136
evaluation, 13
    of flawed wine, 66–67
    savor, 65
    sight, 64
    sip, 65
    slurp, 65
    smell, 64–65
    spitting, 65
    swirl, 64
    training for, 68–69
    in wine-tasting journal, 70–71
    at wine-tasting party, 94–96

Falanghina grapes, 121
Farm Winery Act (1976), 178
fermentation, 51, 58, 193
Fiano grapes, 120
field blends, 117
finish, 70–71
flor, 213
food. *See* pairing food and wine
fortified wines, 14, 60, 82, 89, 208–213
Fournier, Charles, 142
France, 19, 105, 182
    Alsace, 89, 110
    Bordeaux, 114–115, 152–153

Burgundy, 154–155
Chablis, 106–107
Côte Châlonnaise, 108
Côte d'Or, 108–109
Left Bank wines, 152–153
Loire Valley, 112–113, 156–157, 204
Mâconnais, 108–109
red wines, 152–158
Rhône Valley, 114–115, 157–158
Right Bank wines, 152–153
sparkling wines, 192–195
white wines, 114–115
wine-making terms in, 106
Franciacorta, 198–199
Frank, Konstantin, 132, 142
fruit, 13, 69. See also grapes

Gallo, Ernest, 131
Gallo, Julio, 131
Gamay, 24, 154–155
Germany, 105, 207
    red wines, 168
    Riesling from, 124–125
Gewürztraminer, 21
Giovanna, Gunther di, 46
glasses, 91, 95
Glera grapes (Prosecco), 197
Grand Cru vineyards, 105–110, 155, 193
Grange, 186
grapes, 33, 43, 77.
    *See also specific types*
    German regulations on, 124–125
    hybrids of, 38, 142–143
    table, 13
grappa, 55
Greco grapes, 120
Greece, 127
Grenache/Garnacha, 24, 157
grower-producers (Récoltant-Manipulant) (RM), 195
growing seasons, 27
    harvest, 30
    spring, 28
    summer, 29
Grüner Veltliner, 21, 126

Halliday, James, 186

Harazthy, Agoston, 132
health, 18–19, 79, 91
horizontal tasting, 96
humidity, 84
Hungary, 127, 207
Hussman, George, 128

ice wine, 207
importers, 78
Inglenook, 128
Integrated Pest Management (IPM), 46
Internet buying, 100
IPM. *See* Integrated Pest Management
Italy, 105
    Central, 118–119, 162–163
    dessert wines, 206
    islands, 121, 164, 206
    Lombardia, 198–199
    Northeast, 116–117, 162
    Northwest, 114, 116, 161
    Piedmont, 199, 206
    red wines, 161–164
    Soave, 117
    Southern, 120–121, 164
    Trentino, 199
    Trentino-Alto Adige, 116–117
    Tuscany, 206
    Valle d'Aosta, 116
    Veneto, 117, 197, 206
IVBAM. *See* Embroidery and Handicraft Institute of Madeira

Jefferson, Thomas, 128
Judgment of Paris, 131, 174

labels, 98, 104, 120, 193
    in California, 136
    designations on, 76–79
    in Oregon, 141
    popes related to, 158
    vintage-labeled wines, 77, 136, 194, 208–209
Left Bank wines, 152–153
legs, 65
Lett, David, 174
Loire Valley, 112–113, 156–157, 204
Lombardia, 198–199

South Africa, 150–151, 190
Spain, 105, 123, 212–213
    red wines, 167
    regulations in, 122
    sparkling wines, 201
sparkling carbonated wine, 14, 34
sparkling wines, 56–57, 64, 89, 91,
    147. *See also specific types*
        France, 192–195
        New World, 202–203
        Old World, 192–201
        opening, 92–93
        United States, 202–203
        vintage of, 58
Steiner, Rudolph, 47
Stevenson, Tom, 47
storing, 84–86
sugar, 124, 204. *See also* dessert wines;
    sweetness
sugar to, 125
sulfites, 51, 79
sulfur dioxide, 51, 66
sunlight, 84
Sunny St. Helena Winery, 133
sustainable winemaking, 47, 177
sweetness, 73, 194–195. *See also*
    dessert wines
Switzerland, 127
Syrah grapes, 157, 177

Tank Method (Charmat Method), 56,
    197
Tannat, 183
tannin, 69, 73, 82
Tasmania, 147
taste, 65, 82
        pairing food and wine for, 72–73
        training palate for, 68–69
        turned wine and, 84–85
        in wine-tasting journal, 70–71
        in wine-tasting party, 94–96
tawny port, 209
Tchelistcheff, André, 133
temperature, 17, 44, 48, 84, 211
Tempranillo, 25, 167
terroir, 34. *See also* soil
themes, 95
Thompson Seedless grapes, 131

Tokaj (Hungary), 207
Trebbiano, 22
Trentino, 199
truffles, 75
Tunisia, 190
Tuscany, 206

United States, 19, 128, 131–133
    California, 95, 134–138,
        170–173, 202–203
    classified growing areas in,
        104–105
    market in, 104
    New Mexico, 203
    New York, 142, 178, 203
    Oregon, 140, 174
    red wines, 170–179
    single vineyard wines in, 105
    sparkling wines, 202–203
    Washington state, 141, 177
    white wines, 134–143
Uruguay, 183

Valle d'Aosta, 116
Veneto, 117, 197, 206
Verdejo grapes, 123
vermouth, 60
    as aromatized, 208
vertical tasting, 96
Victoria (Australia), 186
vines, 132
age of, 31, 40–41
diseases of, 42–43
roots of, 31, 38, 40
species of, 38–39
understanding, 32–37
vineyards, 40–41, 105. *See also specific
    vineyards*
Grand Cru, 106–107, 155, 193
premier cru, 105, 108, 155, 193
vintage, 58, 60
vintage-labeled wines, 77, 136, 194,
    208–209
Viognier, 22, 136, 138
volume, of wine bottles, 78–79

warnings, 18–19, 79
Washington state, 141, 177

water, 34, 37, 148, 188
weather and rain, 34, 37, 44, 121, 148,
    188. *See also specific locations*
white grapes, 20–22. *See also specific
    white grapes; specific white wines*
white still wine, 14
white wines, 50–51, 58, 82
    Australia, 146–147
    Austria, 126–127
    California, 134–138
    Chablis, 74, 106–107
    France, 114–115
    New World, 134–151
    New Zealand, 148–149
    South Africa, 150–151
    United States, 134–143
wine, 13
    by-products of, 55
    calories in, 19
    cooking with, 75
    filtration of, 53
    greatness of, 15
    origins of, 33–34
    quality of, 66–67
    types of, 14, 56–57
The Wine Group Inc., 104
winemaking
    aspect in, 36
    biodynamic, 47
    development of, 34
    organic, 46, 145, 177
    slope in, 36
    soil for, 34, 36, 74
    sustainable, 47
    temperatures for, 44, 48
wine-tasting journal, 70–71
wine-tasting party, 94–96
wood barrels, 50, 52–53, 109, 167

yeast, 50–51

Zinfandel, 25, 172